C 708

CW00763563

201

Book + DVD   LOCAL

RETFORD

R. 1. 08

19 FEB 2008

COUNTY LIBRARY

**Nottinghamshire
County Council**

DP&P(O) 08/05/C&C/4261

Please return / renew by the
last date shown.

On Task, On Target

The story of Tuxford School's first fifty years

Nottinghamshire County Council

L37.1 TUXFORD

Culture & Community

Terence W. E. White

Pinnacle Books

First published in Great Britain in 2007 by

Pinnacle Books
49 Pastures Road, Barrowby, Grantham, Lincs. NG32 1BA
Author: Terence W. E. White

Copyright © Terence W. E. White, 2007

All rights reserved. The contents of this publication are the copyright of the
publisher and may not be reproduced, stored in a retrieval system, or transmitted
by any means, without written permission from the publisher. Every care has been
taken to ensure the accuracy of the information contained in this publication, but no
liability can be accepted for any loss or damage whether direct, indirect or
consequential arising out of the use of the information contained herein.

ISBN: 978-0-9556220-0-7

Typeset, designed and printed in Great Britain 2007 by
Tradelink Publications Ltd
www.tradelinkpub.co.uk

Pinnacle Books

Contents

Acknowledgements

The rebuilding of Tuxford School (July 2005 to February 2007) has been an event of such significance for staff and students that it demanded to be recorded. But the original "old" school (built July 1957 to September 1958) was remarkable too in its day and its construction was of national significance. The eagerness of several students from the initial 1958 intake to bid an emotional farewell to their school before demolition, suggested that there could be an audience "out there" for a published History – so here it is.

A successful bid to the now defunct Countryside Agency for Local Heritage Initiative funding, provided the impetus to sign a book contract – and then there was no going back. The official school archives at this point were of little help so assembling a collection of documents and photographs was essential preparation for this book. Thanks to the foresight and enthusiasm of four people, the archives developed swiftly. Tuxford's first Headteacher, Bernie Woodward, had ensured that his papers were preserved by donating them to Bassetlaw Museum in Retford. School Librarian Carole Wall, meticulously saved school-related newscuttings and ephemera after her appointment in 1985. Mollie Whitehead of the school office recognised the historical significance of items that her colleagues regarded as clutter. Finally, teacher Julie Hethershaw preserved hundreds of photographs of school camps, expeditions and trips, thereby enriching the pictorial record of school life.

The staff of Bassetlaw Museum are thanked for granting access to the Woodward Archive and for their untiring support of the school's heritage project. Dick Makin of DK Imaging has made a stunning visual record of the rebuild process; my thanks to him and to his wife Jo for their enthusiastic support. Thanks to the school's publishing team for typing and display support for the project. A special thanks to Carol Brumpton for bubbly optimism and much needed encouragement at times of work pressure – especially during the application for funding.

I am also grateful to Michelle Woolley of Tradelink Publications Ltd for transforming words and images into finished pages; thanks to her for the dedication, skill and patience shown.

Finally, we have included much of the material forming our archive. If you have information, photographs and documents that reveal other aspects of school history, I would much appreciate access to them.

T.W.W.
March 2007

Support from the Local Heritage Intitiative is gratefully acknowledged.

Origins and Founding Principles

Before Tuxford County Secondary School opened in September 1958 most of the older children of the area were educated in the senior classes of their village schools until they attained school leaving age. From 1918 until 1947 the leaving age was 14; in 1947 it was raised to 15. The quality of education provided for the post 11 age group would have been very poor by modern standards because there were not the resources or the specialist teachers in the small schools to provide a broad curriculum. The accommodation would have been poor too. Mrs Elsie Pickering was a junior teacher at Tuxford in 1957 and she recalls how every available space was used including a room at the former Read Grammar School on Lincoln Street, a wooden hut and "a canteen-style building at the bottom of the school field." (1)

It was not until the 1944 Education Act passed into law that local authorities were compelled to provide secondary education for everyone. Before this only two types of education provision in the country were recognised: elementary and higher and whilst local authorities had a duty to provide elementary education for all up to the school leaving age, they did not have to make any other provision. They had discretionary powers to fund secondary schools if they chose to do so, but most chose not to. For eighty per cent of children dedicated secondary schools were not available. At a press conference in June 1960 to launch big increases in spending, the Director of Education for Nottinghamshire, Mr J. Edward Mason, admitted that his county could have done more: "Secondary education

Student at the new school.

The wordwork room.

was not compulsory until after the 1944 Act, and Notts. had lagged behind most counties." (2)

In Tuxford before 1944, there was a "senior school" for the older (post 11) students, but it was not the separate entity that the title suggests. The Newark Advertiser report of the official opening of the County Secondary School, 16 July 1959, tells us that "three former headmasters of Tuxford senior schools" attended: Mr J. Mollart, who was head from 1929 to 1934, Mr G.E. Bates who succeeded him (1934-40) and Mr C.J. Cooper (1940-43). (3) The report could as easily have recorded that these gentlemen were the head teachers of the elementary school. Under their successor, Mr Blackwell, post 11 students were organised into two senior classes: one for pupils aged 11 to 13 and the other for the 13 to 15 age group. As the more academic girls and boys had left for grammar schools at the end of their time in junior class, the curriculum for remaining students took on a vocational bias to prepare them for leaving school. Before the secondary school opened, Tuxford was already offering craft lessons to other schools in the area. Tom Grasby taught woodwork in the wooden hut at the senior school (mentioned above) to Sutton-on-Trent, Normanton and Norwell students from the south of the area as well as to those from Tuxford. When the secondary school opened Tom Grasby was one of the teachers who transferred to it, together with his tools and benches. (See Ivor Nettleton's account of the move, below).

Although it took Nottinghamshire County Council thirteen years to begin building Tuxford's secondary school after the passing of the 1944 Education Act it had a clear strategy for implementing the Act. Section 7 of the Act declared that "The statutory system of public education shall be organised in three progressive stages to be known as primary education, secondary education and further education." The County's response, the Education Development Plan, was published in May 1947. 125 new primary schools would be built, 44 new secondary moderns, 23 new grammar / technical schools, 9 special schools and 181 nursery schools. The Retford Times recorded the Plan's launch in its May 9 edition with some incredulity: "Nearly £20,000,000 is to

£78,000 School for Tuxford

LAST week we were able to give some details of the Notts. Education Committee's development plan as it related to Retford and this week we deal with the committee's proposals as they affect the Tuxford area.

Principal among the plans of the Education Committee is that of the erection of a new county secondary school at Tuxford, to accommodate 300 pupils, at a cost of some £78,000 plus a further £4,200 for a site.

There are four schools to be retained in the Tuxford area – Norwell C.E., E. Markham County, Sutton-on-Trent County and Tuxford County. All these, however, are going to be the subject of considerable alteration and adaptation, together with extensions of sites as follows:

NORWELL C.E.
Conversion of existing building to two classrooms, staff room assembly hall and ancillary...

Reproduced courtesy of the Retford Times. *16 May 1947.*

4

be spent on education in Nottinghamshire in the course of the next few years. This was the staggering revelation made to members of the Notts. County Council on Tuesday…" (4)

The responsibility placed on local councils by the Act was clear: "… it shall be the duty of the local education authority for every area, so far as their powers extend, to contribute towards the spiritual, moral, mental, and physical development of the community by securing that efficient education throughout those stages shall be available to meet the needs of the population of their area." The educational ideals of the Act were supported by Alderman Mrs Wainwright when she seconded the proposal to adopt the Notts. Plan: "We want every child in this county to have the opportunity to develop its talents to the full, that it shall be looked after, irrespective of where it was born, where it lives, the religious beliefs of its parents, or if it has any physical defects. We hope that, in return, our children will give of those talents, when they are required, to the service of the world as a whole."

Elsie Pickering and Colin Maw with group.

It is a common misconception that the 1944 Act introduced selection into education and that it prescribed the establishment of secondary modern schools. It did neither. Entrance exams for many grammar schools dated back to the latter's acceptance of county council grants – and this was in Victorian times for most grammar schools. The impact of the exams on teaching in junior classes of elementary schools could be significant. Mrs Pickering recalls the impact on her teaching: "I was assigned the junior class for pupils aged 9 to 11… Of course I had to focus on preparing for the 11+ so that the more academic students could win places in the grammar schools." As for the types of secondary school built after the Act, the Dukeries School at Ollerton was planned just two years after Tuxford Secondary School opened and it was to be a comprehensive from the start. Nottinghamshire had deliberately embarked on a series of experiments when it began implementing the 1944 Act. Tuxford was an experimental school specialising in serving the rural economy, the "first built on the county's new (CLASP) system, the first with an open-air gymnasium – and the first to keep cows". (3) Ollerton was an experimental comprehensive: organised into houses so its pupils felt part of a small cohesive unit within the larger organisation. J. Edward Mason claimed in a Newark Advertiser article of 8 July 1960 that the school would "set the pattern for a new type of secondary school in Britain." The article also mentioned another county experiment: building a campus of grouped schools "at Calverton, where four separate schools have been built on one campus in the last five years." (5)

The introduction of secondary modern schools (and of senior schools) can be traced back

5

Tuxford County School's 1878 building.

to a report by the Consultative Committee of the Board of Education published in 1926. The Committee under the chairmanship of Sir Henry Hadow was asked to review developments in post primary education within elementary schools. Its report on Education of the Adolescent – known as the Hadow Report – recommended secondary education for all. The Committee felt that educational provision should take account of individual needs and attainments. In small elementary schools there had been no practical alternative to mixed ability teaching – and often delivered to classes catering for more than one year group. It is not surprising that the Hadow Committee deplored the lack of attention for the individual child. Its solution, the most effective way to provide individual learning pathways, was to recommend separate schools for different children.

Grammar schools would cater for students best suited for an academic education and these would "pursue in the main a predominantly literary or scientific curriculum". Modern schools, similar to the central schools developed in London and Manchester from 1911 were to have a commercial or industrial bias, but were not to be narrowly vocational. A third type of provision, technical schools, was recommended to respond to "the needs and requirements of certain local industries." The Report was very influential and its recommendations were adopted in principle – but, as we have noted, few schools were built before the 1944 Act compelled local authorities to take action. In the meantime most councils focused on another Hadow recommendation: that if the creation of separate secondary schools were not possible, senior classes should be established in elementary schools to provide a better focused education for post primary students. This was the option chosen for Tuxford. Senior schools were in effect low quality secondary moderns because the students in them were those who had not been selected for grammar schools.

The Hadow Report stressed that all types of secondary school should have equal status and all could apply selection processes if desired. When Tuxford's new school opened in 1958, the press coverage - which was extensive - was very positive and encouraging. Instead of focusing on what early Tuxford students were not (academic high fliers) the papers emphasised the important role of the school in developing good citizens and responsible workers in important industries such as farming and mining. A Retford Times article of August 1959 provides an interesting insight into attitudes at the time so it is reproduced below in edited form. (6) The writer clearly approved of the school's founding principles "Tuxford's Secondary School is an experiment and one that is, without a shadow of a doubt, well on the way to succeeding. But the essence of the Tuxford school, among so much that is new, is the freedom given to the individual child and also the trust reposed in them". A number of interviews with early students, arranged as preparation for this book, reveal that from the start Tuxford County Secondary School was a happy place: popular with parents, well run and based in high quality accommodation. It was self-assured

Reading and needlework.

and proud: not believing itself inferior to a grammar school. However, nationally, it was not long before the wisdom of creating two types of secondary schools was questioned. By 1965 Tuxford's first headteacher, Mr B. W. Woodward, was aware of the injustices of selection and he sought to defend his pupils' reputations. He proudly announced at the annual Prizegiving that a number of Tuxford's pupils had transferred to other schools and were taking 'A' level subjects. "These are pupils who were judged to be 11-plus failures," he said. (7)

At the time of writing, in 2007, grammar schools and secondary modern schools still exist in parts of the United Kingdom – notably in Lincolnshire. The grammar schools are often long-established, with a proud tradition of producing leaders of industry, top civil servants, university luminaries and senior officers in the armed services. In contrast, the remaining secondary modern schools often style themselves as "high schools" or even as "comprehensives" (in spite of many or most of the more academically gifted students in their catchment areas being selected to attend grammar schools).

Selective schools disappeared from most of the United Kingdom, including Nottinghamshire, during the 1960s and 1970s. The process of reorganisation sparked impassioned debate between advocates and opponents of selection and often the language used by both sides was emotive. Supporters of grammar schools felt – and still feel – that intellectual development is faster within highly competitive single sex environments which are free from populist low brow distractions and "yobbish" tendencies. Opponents point out that the cost of selecting twenty or thirty per cent of students for grammar schools is that seventy or eighty per cent of secondary age students are left with a deeply ingrained sense of failure from the age of eleven. On one side selection is seen as nothing more sinister than a logical extension of streaming; on the other it is viewed as "educational apartheid" creating social groups unable to understand each other. The opponents of selection won the argument in Parliament and in most councils so the system was changed.

We shall examine later the process by which Tuxford County Secondary School became a comprehensive from 1st September 1976. The school had enjoyed a good reputation as a secondary modern and this was sustained when its status changed.

Sources

1. *Mr Woodward's School*, Elsie Pickering, Tuxford School Archive Papers, unpublished, 2005
2. *Education Budget in Notts.*, Retford Times, 24 June 1960
3. *Tuxford's new school has its own farm*, Newark Advertiser, 22 July 1959
4. *Council's £19,358,475 Education Plan*, Retford Times, 9 May 1947
5. *Comprehensive idea in Notts.*, Newark Advertiser, 8 July 1960
6. *The Very Model of an Ultra-Model School*, Retford Times, 21 August 1959
7. *Discuss education, parents urged*, Newark Advertiser, 16 October 1965

Secondary school aims explained

PARENTS of every child in Nottinghamshire due to transfer to a secondary school after the summer holidays are this year receiving, a personal message from the County Director of Education, Mr. J. Edward Mason.

Commenting on the different types of school, he writes: "Secondary modern schools are undoubtedly the ones in which the great majority of children can best learn.

"The pupils may legally leave at the end of the term in which they reach their 15th birthday, but the committee are convinced that it is necessary in the interests of all pupils to remain until the end of their fourth year and to take the Nottinghamshire Leaving Certificate examination.

"The subjects taught in secondary modern schools are similar to those taken in grammar and technical schools, but they are approached in a different way and suited to the very varying abilities of the children.

The aim

"The aim of any secondary school is to give a good general education in English, mathematics, science, art, social studies, music, physical and religious education, as well as practical subjects such as homecrafts, needlework and the crafts of wood and metal.

"The secondary modern school tries to discover the best in every pupil and to develop this through interesting practical work leading to advances in other subjects as a natural consequence.

Mr. Mason points out that the allocation of children to different schools really starts, not with the "11-plus examination" but at the age of seven.

"Many parents are sure in their own minds to which school they consider their children should go, but the person who can help most is the primary school head," he says.

Watched

"Many parents, however, know little of what the committee does to be equally sure, and believe the competitive scholarship procedure of pre-war years still prevails. "From the age of seven onwards, the pupils in the primary school are studied and take part, often unknown to themselves, in tests which carefully measure their ability and their attainments.

"In the last year of work at the primary school, the head teacher is asked to give his opinion. Even this is rechecked again by a further series of tests and consultations with individual records.

Reproduced courtesy of the *Newark Advertiser.* 15 June 1960.

The 1958 Building:

An Award-winning Prototype

The groundbreaking new school.

For various reasons a major school building programme was needed at the end of the Second World War. Not only had five thousand schools been destroyed by enemy bombs, but also four out of five elementary schools – many in rural areas and run by voluntary bodies - were considered inadequate or unfit and in need of remodelling or replacing. For the previous five years investment had gone into the war effort and for many schools the only construction was the provision of bomb shelters so a deterioration in the fabric of most schools had to be addressed. The school leaving age was also raised in 1947. The creation of separate secondary schools, as required by the 1944 Education Act, added to the financial strain felt by local authorities. (At the same time they needed to recruit and train 70,000 additional teachers). Nevertheless councils had to meet their obligations and the government required them to publish development plans. It took until the end of 1947 for 126 LEAs out of 146 to prepare their plans. Nottinghamshire's Plan was presented to the county council on 6 May 1947.

Included in the 1947 LEA Plan was a secondary school for Tuxford. It was envisaged that purchase of a site would cost £4,200 and that £78,000 would be needed for construction. However, Tuxford would have to wait its turn. Dunham and Elkesley were to get brand new primary schools; Norwell, East Markham, Sutton-on-Trent and Tuxford primary schools were to be extended and improved. Other local primary schools would simply close at specified

9

Interiors

Mr Forster in the library.

The sports barn.

PE laundry for washing kit.

dates as they were considered unviable: Carlton-on-Trent, Egmanton and Laxton in 1951; Bothamsall, East Drayton and West Markham in 1958; Weston in 1959. Normanton-on-Trent CofE School was also due for the axe in 1959, but it continues to thrive today. (1)

Of course, schools couldn't simply appear overnight. Realistic planning had to prioritise reconstruction projects and so stopgap measures such as opening a temporary secondary school at Flintham in former RAF huts were tried. The emphasis immediately after the war was placed on primary schools. We should remember that major reconstruction was needed in all areas of national life, from large scale housing to whole town centres, so funding of education had to compete with other spending needs. Traditional building materials and skilled craftsmen to use them were in short supply due to the huge demand and this pushed up costs. As a short term measure temporary buildings were installed throughout the country: so called "HORSA" huts (Hut Operation Raising School-leaving Age). Tuxford primary school had one of these as noted above. As a long term solution planners and architects were encouraged to explore alternative construction methods: to drive down costs at the same time as speeding up the actual building process. Steel frames and prefabricated panels were a possible solution.

Modern methods had been tried in various places before the war, notably in Middlesex and West Sussex. In 1937 the News Chronicle had run a competition inviting designs for the ideal school, and the winning design made good use of space, light and modern materials - as have hundreds of schools since then. After the war Hertfordshire gained a reputation for being at the forefront of design innovation. However, Nottinghamshire too came to play a prominent role in promoting reliable and cheap industrialised building methods nationwide - and Tuxford Secondary School was held up as a model building for other authorities to copy.

Hertfordshire is directly relevant to our story because the team of talented young architects assembled in that county after the war went on to influence both government planning policy and the design principles that were put into practice. The challenge of building fast and cheap was successfully addressed there earlier than most other places because it experienced a population explosion from the London overspill (and the creation of four new towns: Hemel Hempstead, Stevenage, Welwyn Garden City and Hatfield). A grid design system was adopted by the team: in simple terms a square of graph paper translated into a standard span in a building. Corridors and rooms could vary in height, width and layout, but the components were always the standard length. All steelwork and panels could be ordered in bulk and then used in any building designed using the same grid. The schools that emerged had an immediate impact - as summarised by Stuart Maclure writing in 1984: "They looked unlike any other schools which most people had ever seen... The use of large areas of glass, the flat roofs, the bold colours, the impression of openness and lavish space – all contributed to the impact." (2) The success of the design concept was not difficult to quantify. The Hertfordshire Buildings Committee had estimated that a medium sized school would take three and a quarter years to build by traditional methods, but the industrialised building process reduced the time needed by two and a half years.

Ten years before Tuxford School was built Hertfordshire had already solved many of the problems of mass production within the building industry. The relevance for Tuxford is that Hertfordshire-trained architects went on to hold prominent positions elsewhere and some had a significant influence on the building programme in Nottinghamshire. After one deputy county architect for Herts., Stirrat Johnson-Marshall, became chief architect of the Ministry of Education (from 1948 to 1956) he was joined by four of his former colleagues from

ON "SPRINGS"

school aims explained

The ai...

CHEAPER COST IN
SUBSIDENCE AREAS

DAILY TELEGRAPH REPORTER

A new building system for
schools has been adopted by
eight local authorities in
Britain. On their present programme they aim to put up 31
schools for nearly £500,000 less
than the ceiling figure of the
Ministry of Education.

The method of...

"The aim of an...
school is to give a g
education in Engl
matics, science,
studies, music, phy
religious education,
pract...

PARENTS of ever...
Nottingh...
transfer...
sch...

Notts. Schools will be Foremost of Their Kind

How Pupils will Train at Misterton and Tuxford

MISTERTON Rural County Secondary School, to be opened on May 6th, will be the foremost of its kind in the country for the purpose for which it was specifically designed—training pupils in the pursuit and love of rural subjects.

What is more, Tuxford Rural Secondary Modern School, the building of which is to be started within weeks and due to be completed inside 12 months, will be the equal of the Misterton School in all its aspects and wide scope.

Misterton will find room for 240 pupils, while Tuxford will have a total of 360 at first, but it is most likely that this number will be extended quite quickly.

Both these schools are an entirely new departure from the old-fashioned concepts of the traditional village school.

As rural Secondary Modern Schools their aim will be to give a sound general education and to combine this with a vocational interest, particularly during the final two years of the pupils' life at school.

One outstanding feature of the schools will be the large amount of open space in relation to the buildings themselves.

Misterton, for instance, with six classrooms and seven practical rooms, stands on a 14-tical rooms. The extra space will...

in certain cases a range of agricultural and practical rooms has been provided to form a farm wing. These include live-stock sheds and poultry houses, wood and metalwork shops, and rooms for domestic economy. Subjects which are related to each other are sited near each other; thus housecraft and needlework rooms, science laboratory, the garden room and the greenhouse, metal and woodwork rooms and the farm wing are designed as inter-related units.

This helps the study and de-velopment of the different sub-jects, is a great saver of the teachers' time and energy, and assists preparations and demon-strations.

Where possible, additional land is acquired for the de-velopment of agricultural and horticultural studies. Tools and materials, including livestock, shrubs, trees and plants, are provided, to encourage the de-velopment of exciting and in-spiring education schemes which use the background of the Nottinghamshire country-side.

In connection with the new at Misterton, approval has been given for juniors and following primary reorganisa-...

Senior pupils will also transfer to the new Misterton School from Clayworth County Junior Mixed and Infants School.

Previously, senior pupils hav transferred to Secondar Schools in Retford.

Senior pupils from Evert County Primary School v also be included.

Nottinghamshire Educa Committee are grateful to Retford Rural District Cou for the help they have in assisting with housin school staff.

Estimated to cost i region of £111,520 the b of the new County Sec School at Ordsall Hall is be started in the autu will be completed w year.

An outstanding fe this school will be th ing beauty of its se of which many of the oldest and most Universities would b

No plans are er the moment by N tion Committee are the Ordsall Villa School.

The position w proposed extens' Harworth-Bircote that the Minist tion's decision is it is thought

Reproduced courtesy of the *Retford Times*. Date unknown, possibly April 1957.

On Task, On Target *The story of the first fifty years of Tuxford School*

that county – and in 1955 two more of their old team, W. Dan Lacey and Henry Swain, moved to Nottinghamshire. The Herts. influence meant that in the ministry senior staff were promoting modern building methods and they were predisposed to look favourably on Nottinghamshire's developments. (Another deputy county architect for Hertfordshire, W. Tatton Brown, became the chief architect for the Ministry of Health. A third team member became chief architect of the Ministry of Housing).

The Nottinghamshire County Architect who recruited Lacey and Swain was Donald Gibson who had already achieved great distinction for planning the rebuilding of Coventry city centre after the infamous bombing raids of 1940. The task that he set his new staff was to devise a safe but cheap method of building on land in former mining areas liable to subsidence. To free the staff in his department from their routine workload so they could focus on the task he persuaded councillors to employ private architects for all school building projects in the 1956/57 financial year. What emerged from that year of research and development was not only the design for Tuxford School, but also the building system used to construct many other schools throughout the UK in the following decade. (3)

Thirteen systems were tested by the team and shortcomings were found in all of them. However the system used to build a school in Belper had potential so the Nottinghamshire architects decided to work with the steel company that had supplied the framework for that school, Brockhouse Steel Structures of West Bromwich, to refine the concept. The key features of the system developed were a light steel frame, pin jointed to permit movement, mounted on a five inch slab of concrete cast in sections and reinforced with mesh so it too could adjust to changing ground conditions. The steel frame incorporated diagonal spring-loaded steel braces that could respond to movement underneath or to strong wind or heavy loading. All the innovative features, as a combined package, became known as the Nottinghamshire "Rock and Roll" building system – and the design for Tuxford was based on it even though there was no risk of subsidence in the area. Intake Farm Infants School, Mansfield was the prototype and it opened in September 1957, but Tuxford was the prototype multi-storey building and construction began in July 1957. Both school buildings received national news coverage.

Before we focus on the school at Tuxford it is interesting to note the process by which the "Rock and Roll" system became widespread. The Ministry approached Nottinghamshire to suggest that its system should be shared with other counties that were subject to subsidence and the county didn't need much persuading as it had already realised that the cost per ton of steel components could be reduced significantly by placing combined orders with other authorities. A consortium was duly formed. The Consortium of Local Authorities Special Programme (CLASP) had Coventry, Derbyshire, Durham, Glamorgan, the West Riding of Yorkshire and Leicester as founder members alongside Nottinghamshire. Donald Gibson was chairman and he remained in that position when he moved from his county job in 1958 to become Director General of Works for the War Office because he brought his ministry into CLASP as a full member. Dan Lacey replaced Gibson as Nottinghamshire County Architect until 1964 when he became Chief Architect to the Department for Education and Science.

Returning to Tuxford, the first requirement for the new secondary school was a site. Former teacher Mrs Liz Bradshaw, a native of the town, recalled in 2005, "The land the school stands on belonged to George Capps. I believe that it was compulsorily purchased and it was rumoured that the stress of the sale exacerbated his already delicate health so that he died soon after in his stockyard. The land now occupied by the playing field had always suffered

View from the hall to the quadrangle.

Canopy over footpath leading from garden room into the main corridor.

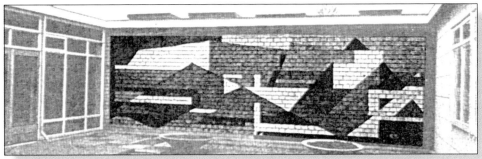

Dorothy Annan Mural.

from drainage problems as it is heavy clay and had been ploughed by my father when he did contract work for Mr Capps. Going back even further, I have heard a suggestion that school was originally intended for a site off Ollerton road." The validity of the rumours would be difficult if not impossible to establish. Suffice it to say that George Capps is still revered in Tuxford as the founder of a charitable trust administered jointly by the vicar and parish council chairman. In addition to the school site, some of his land was purchased for housing and a very modest street in the housing estate to the west of the school is named after him. A large government site on the Ollerton road was sold in November 1960 - after the school had been built: the militia camp used as an army training centre both during the war and after. The 22 acre site, British Fields, was bought by a Yorkshire businessman and later much of it was sold on to Walkers Storage. Other land on the same road but closer to the town centre has been developed since. However any site on Ollerton road would have been a considerable walking distance away from the homes of most Tuxford children.

The design for the school was largely ready by October 1956. The two members of Gibson's team who drew up the plan were L.H. Blockley and A. Goodman and the amendments panel included in the December 1956 update of the drawing, indicates that their focus was on toilets and storage by that time. Another interesting aspect of the plan was that it included proposed future extensions to the building. Across the courtyard from the main three storey block it was envisaged that a second corridor would be built parallel to the one passing the main entrance (connecting the hall to the rural studies room). A Music / rehearsal room would go approximately where the drama studio later was situated. Between it and the housecraft (later food) room would be another housecraft room and across the new corridor would be a room for history / geography and another for science.

The contractors appointed for the construction were Messrs Sweeney and Palmer of Aspley, Nottingham. An artist was commissioned to design a mural for the courtyard between the hall and changing rooms. (The space was later roofed over and turned into another classroom, PE1. Dorothy Annan's work is still exhibited today in various city art galleries including Brighton, Leicester and Manchester so the mural was not merely intended to be decorative; it was an attempt to bring art to the masses. However, the location was not well-considered and the courtyard paving was out of harmony with the brightly-coloured geometric patterns that Annan created. (The exciting mural was never fully appreciated by the school and it was not even recorded for posterity before being covered by wall panels to create PE1). Whether the mural was valued before destruction is unknown).

Children landscaping in the amphitheatre.

Brockhouse Steel Structures, a major components supplier to the CLASP consortium, undertook to produce a promotional film, 'On Schedule', to record all stages of construction. Its soundtrack provides interesting details and insights: "This school, at Tuxford, has been planned with teaching units radiating around the school centre, which consists of entrance hall, library, dining room and assembly hall. The science, woodwork, art and housecraft rooms are at one end of the school centre with the gymnasium, covered practice area and changing rooms at the other... The gym with its excellent wall finish of pirana pine has a covered practice area beyond made possible in the budget by the economies effected by the building method. The teaching block over the library is fully glazed at the front and back and has attractive tile cladding on the other two sides. Access is by two staircases, which, like the remainder of the building, have been assembled on site from standard factory-produced components.

"The site is levelled and consolidated with a vibratory roller. A bed of sand or shale is laid and consolidated to give a smooth surface upon which the concrete raft will be cast. There are no foundations in the ground... Pre-fabricated roof decks, six foot eight inches or ten foot long, are nailed into position as soon as the steel work has been erected. They form a continuous diaphragm that keeps the steelwork square in plan and transmits wind forces to the diagonal bracing. Erection of this roof took four men only four days. Bitumen coating and finishing took only three days more..." (5)

First headteacher Bernard Woodward itemised the costs of building the school in an information leaflet for parents. The total cost of the school, £107,084, was made up of £13,066 for playing fields, external works and caretaker's cottage, £91,768 for the school buildings and £2,250 for the farm unit. Mr Woodward proudly pointed out that the whole project was delivered £10,000 under budget because £117,396 had been set aside. The cost was £256 per pupil in the first intake including all fitted furniture and playgrounds or 68s/2d (£3.41) per square foot. He was impressed by some of the design details: "It is a CLASP building, having a light flexible steel frame, without traditional foundations. It makes use of red tiling and black boarding externally as these materials are in sympathy with the farm buildings in this county. The internal partitions are prefabricated plaster panels and the floor finishes are mainly woodblock and plastic tiles with rubber on upper floors."

For approximately five years after it opened, Tuxford County Secondary School played host to many visitors, both British and foreign, who came to study the building. Journalists, government representatives or education officials from Spain, Turkey, Rhodesia, Sudan, Basutoland and Laos were shown around – and delegates from all over the world attending a Commonwealth conference visited as a group. The High Sheriff of Nottingham even chose the school as the venue for an official Garden Party in July 1959. The Daily Mirror carried an editorial praising school design and chose Tuxford as its example of excellence. In March 1960 Mr Woodward was interviewed by The Times Educational Supplement together with the head of another new school. The interviewer tried to provoke him into being critical, but Mr Woodward would not be drawn:

"Mr Woodward, turning to your own school, Tuxford, would you say that it is 'friendly and informal' …?

"Mr Woodward: I think that the overall plan of Tuxford does in fact lend this informality to every sphere of activity within the school, and that staff do not feel that there is any problem with supervision. The whole scope of teaching is changing as a result of educational planning with a body of teachers, members of staff of the education department, together with county planning authorities.

"Are there any disadvantages of this scattered layout? It has been said that it must take an awful long time to walk from one end of the building to the other.

"Mr Woodward: No. As a result of the fifth term of operation we have found no great

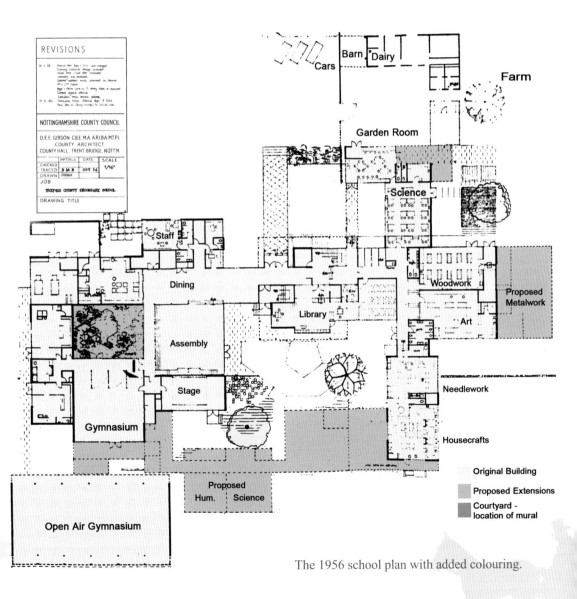

The 1956 school plan with added colouring.

17

An aerial view of the 1958 building.

disadvantages; in fact, all staff are in favour of this system. I have sounded them on this: they find it ideal from the point of view of classroom movement and corridor movement.

"What do you feel about the aesthetics of Tuxford? One distinguished architect has called it "messy and chi-chi."

"Mr Woodward: I see round every corner beautiful features." (6)

Six years later former Tuxford teacher Gordon Ellis was more analytical when writing a dissertation on 'School Design' submitted to the University of Nottingham in July 1966. He admitted that design faults had become apparent to staff:

"(a) Access to the teaching block is by a poorly thought out stairway system.

(b) The classrooms are not large enough… Their size does not permit free movement.

(c) Paths around the school are far too narrow and their edges ill-defined. Consequently the grassed areas are walked on and become bald, and in wet weather are soon churned up. The resulting mud is taken into school no matter how close the supervision. There ought to have been an old fashioned playground easily reached from the amphitheatre area.

(d) The school field slopes towards the main buildings and after periods of wet weather this slope soon becomes an unsightly morass. A greatly improved drainage system is required to prevent this.

(e) Any use of the main hall for Drama, Oral English, Music or Television lessons is affected by the proximity of the kitchen. The noise and smell… can cause some distraction and inconvenience.

(f) There is no room set aside for careers interviews or quiet work by children.

(g) Storage space is poorly planned and inadequate in some areas.

(h) The car parking area for staff and visitors is woefully inadequate, and dangerous congestion sometimes results." (8)

Not in the list but mentioned elsewhere in the dissertation is another criticism: "In all (rooms) the thermostat is above the heater and not in what could be the coldest part of the room. So the thermostat operates when the air nearest to the heater reaches the desired temperature, and not when the general temperature of the room is that which is required."

Despite listing a few aspects of the building that could be improved Gordon Ellis was generally impressed by it and the impact it was having on the children: "These irritating faults disappear to a certain extent when the building as a whole is considered. It has been designed with children in mind, it is aesthetically pleasing and within its walls a free and responsible community is developing."

The Guardian Journal for 30 October 1959 carried the following item: "The Nottinghamshire County Council Architect, Mr. William D. Lacey, has been awarded the RIBA bronze medal for the best building in the area of the Nottingham, Derby and Lincoln Society of Architects between January 1956 and December 1958…

"The medal will be presented at a dinner-dance of the Nottingham, Derby and Lincoln Society of Architects in December. At the same time a diploma will be presented to the contractors, Sweeney and Palmer, and a plaque for the school will be presented to the chairman of the County Council, Ald. W. Bayliss."

Although this was characterised as a personal success for Lacey, it was, in fact, a major accomplishment for the county team. Their professional peers had concluded that in designing Tuxford School the team had created a building of distinction: one of the best to be built in the East Midlands during a three year period. As is so often the case, the team leader got all the credit but the contribution of Gibson, Swain, Blockley and Goodman should be acknowledged too. Swain certainly played a major role in winning an international architectural prize for CLASP at Milan in 1960. A replica of Barnby Road Primary School, Newark was built there as the British entry – and it won. However, in the following June (1961) it was Lacey who received a CBE in the Queen's Birthday Honours.

A different kind of headline threatened the future of CLASP in 1974. Serious health and safety issues within the building system were discovered in that year because a fire at an old people's home in Edwalton killed 18 people. Cavities in walls and ceilings at the home had permitted smoke and toxic gases to spread too quickly and the use of fixing membranes with a lower fire resistance than the panels being retained allowed the fire to spread. An official enquiry following the tragedy resulted in simple design modifications to ensure that loss of life could not happen again. The remedy satisfied both the experts and the general public so there was no lasting loss of confidence in the building system.

According to Mr Woodward, writing in his 'Retirement Reminiscences' of 1978, the 1958 building was designed with a life expectancy of twenty years. (7) In the event it continued in use for forty nine years and the building stood up well to the wear and tear of passing years. Some people reported that the building had leaned slightly from being upright, but others felt that this was just an illusion. Renovation work at different times included replacing

The 'Best New Building' award from the Royal Institute of British Architects.

Bronze Medal Award for School Design

THE R.I.B.A. bronze medal has been awarded to Mr. William D. Lacy. Notts County Council architect, for the design of the new secondary school at Tuxford.

It is the first multi-storied building constructed by a new method which has been developed to meet the needs of the county council's building programmes.

The school was opened in September last year with 350 pupils.

Reproduced courtesy of the *Retford Times*, 6 Nov 1959.

C.B.E. for Notts. Schools Architect

THE architect who has designed many of Notts. modern schools, including the Tuxford Secondary Modern, has been awarded the C.B.E, in the Queen's Birthday Honours list published on Saturday.

He is Mr. W. D. Lacey, of Radcliffe-on-Trent, the Notts. County Council Architect.

Mr. Lacey, who is married, came to Notts. from Hertfordshire in August, 1955, as senior architect to the County Architect at that time, Mr. Donald Gibson.

On Mr. Gibson's joining the War Office in 1958, Mr. Lacey was promoted.

During his term as County Architect, Mr. Lacey has gained a country-wide reputation and in 1959 he was awarded the RIBA bronze medal for the best building in the area of the Nottingham, Derby and Lincoln Society of Architects for his design of Tuxford Secondary building constructed by a new method.

Mr. Lacey also designed the school which Nottinghamshire County Council exhibited at the Milan Triennial Exhibition in Italy in 1959.

Others in the East Midlands area who have been honoured are: Mr. Frank William Richardson (M.B.E.), of Bleasby, who has been connected with district committees of the Notts. County Agricultural Committee Since 1939.

Mrs. Annie Eleanor Marsh, of Alfred Street, Gainsborough (M.B.E.) for services in connection with the women'a section of the British Legion, both the Gainsborough branch and the East Midlands area.

Mr. W. R. Collier, Chief Engineer, Naval Section, Rose Bros., Gainsborough (M.B.E.) Warrant Officer, Class 1, Mr. Douglas Harris, Army Physical Training Corps, Worksop (M.B.E.. Military). Squadron-Ldr. George Curry, D.F.M., of Blyth (M.B.E., Military).

Extract courtesy of The Retford Times. 16 June 1961.

the wooden weatherboarding and window frames with modern materials, but the overall maintenance costs were modest.

The county council conducted an evaluation of the design in the 1970s by re-examining all CLASP buildings in the county constructed between 1957 and 1971. It discovered that subsidence had occurred 128 times under 70 buildings – but the buildings had only sustained damage totalling £3,288. This vindicated the confidence of the original design team. (8)

The name by which the 1958 building was known changed over the years. When a Lower School block was built in 1976 the original building became known as Main School. During its final years in the new millennium it was known as the Sherwood Building. However, at its heart there was always the award-winning, much discussed innovative "tower block."

Sources

1   *£78,000 School for Tuxford. Retford Times*, 16 May 1947

2   *Education Development & School Building 1945-73*, Stuart Maclure, Longman, 1984, p.54.

3   *Education Development & School Building 1945-73*, Stuart Maclure, Longman, 1984, pp.100-108

4   *Tuxford Beginnings*, Liz Bradshaw (née Fox), Tuxford School Archive Papers, unpublished, 2005

5   *On Schedule*, Saga Films, 1959

6   *Consumer Report, Times Educational Supplement,* 11 March 1960

7   *School Design*, G.P. Ellis, a dissertation for Diploma in Education, University of Nottingham, 1966

8   *Retirement Reminiscences*, Bernard Woodward, Festina Lente school magazine, 1978

9   *Education Development & School Building 1945-73*, Stuart Maclure, Longman, 1984, p.104

Tuxford School Opening

NOTTINGHAMSHIRE COUNTY COUNCIL
EDUCATION COMMITTEE

Official Opening

TUXFORD COUNTY SECONDARY
SCHOOL

On THURSDAY, 16th JULY, 1959, at 3 p.m.
at the School

Admit........Mr. Stanniland & Lady........

Guests are requested to be in their seats by 2.45 p.m.
Seats will not be kept after that time.
This ticket should be shown at the door, and given up later in the tea room

Performing the opening ceremony on Thursday was Mr. Dougles Kennedy. O.B.E. director of the English Folk Dance and Song Society.

Mr Kennedy praised the school and told parents: "The gymnasium and outdoor gymnasium are important because I am also on the side of physical literacy because one should not only be able to think and speak but to be able to move with grace-even if only to get out of the way of a car."

"Perfect school"

He said: "I take it I am speaking on behalf of you all when I say we are here to celebrate a great undertaking-the school is perfect in every way from the functional point of view." ...

OFFICIAL OPENING OF THE

TUXFORD COUNTY SECONDARY SCHOOL

by DOUGLAS KENNEDY, Esq., O.B.E.,
(Director of the English Folk Dance and Song Society)
on Thursday, 16th July at 3 p.m.

PROGRAMME

The Vice-Chairman of the County Council will call upon THE CHAIRMAN OF THE EAST RETFORD RURAL DISTRICT COUNCIL, Councillor E. W. Leckenby, J.P., to speak a few words of welcome.

Item by the pupils of the School.

The Vice-Chairman of the County Council will invite DOUGLAS KENNEDY, ESQ., O.B.E., to deliver his address.

MR KENNEDY will speak and declare the School open.

The Chairman of the Education Committee will propose a vote of thanks.

The Chairman of the School Governing Body, COUNTY COUNCILLOR S. S. HOUSLEY, J.P., will second the vote of thanks.

The Director of Education will support.

The Headmaster will speak.

Prayer of Dedication by THE REV. J. R. N. HOOKER.

The National Anthem.

The School will be open for inspection after the ceremony.
The first tea will be served in the dining area at the conclusion of the programme, and the second, thirty minutes later.

SCHOOL

On THURSDAY, 16th JULY, 1959, at 3 p.m.
at the School

... After the headmaster, Mr. Woodward, had spoken a prayer of dedication was said by the Rev. J. R. N. Hooker.

Present at the opening ceremony were three former head masters of Tuxford senior schools-Mr. J. Mollart. who was head from 1929 to 1934, Mr E. Bates, who succeeded him and Mr. C. Cooper.

After the opening ceremony the schools head boy, 15 years-old Alan Bett, of Darlton, presented Mr. Kennedy with a nut bowl made by 15-years-old Thomas Priestley.

Extracts courtesy of the *Newark Advertiser*. 16 July 1959.

Early Staff and Staffing

Bernard Woodward BSc.
Tuxford School's first headteacher.

The first headteacher of Tuxford School, Bernard Woodward, took up post in May 1958, but he was appointed some time before that date because he was named as the prospective head in a Retford Times news item of 14 February 1958: Tuxford's New Secondary School "On Schedule". At that time he was Deputy Head of a split-site "Grammar / Modern School" in Chipping Norton, Oxfordshire. In effect he was head of the secondary modern part of a larger school catering for the full ability range. He had the necessary experience to realise that the tasks facing him in Tuxford after appointment would be daunting: to liaise with education officials and architects to ensure that the building, its services and transport arrangements would be ready on time, to analyse curriculum needs and to recruit appropriate staff to deliver both curriculum and management, to purchase all books and materials after consultation with newly appointed colleagues, to prepare the first intake by publishing session times, uniform requirements, etc before the summer holiday and to prepare and publish the teaching timetable. However, there was much tighter LEA control over schools in the 1950s and 1960s than today so Mr Woodward would have been carefully guided throughout and his ability to take decisions independently of county would be severely restricted.

Until recently very little was known about Mr Woodward's background. A far from probing interview for the school magazine, Festina Lente, published in July 1978 just prior to his retirement, reveals that photography was a hobby and that he followed both football and cricket "though he doesn't play them now." (1) Two places where he had worked before moving to Tuxford are mentioned: Chipping Norton in the Cotswold Hills and an unknown place in the Vale of Evesham. During the interview he recalled an incident from 1939 when he was teaching in the Vale of Evesham. There was an air raid practice and "everybody scattered into the trees." Other meagre facts that have been known about the first headteacher are: he was aged 43 when he took up his appointment in Nottinghamshire, his teaching subject was geography (by a remarkable coincidence, all three headteachers who have led Tuxford School to date have been geographers) and he lived on London Road, Retford with his wife and family. No personnel record for him exists in school and there is not even an official portrait in the archives. However thanks to his foresight Mr Woodward's official correspondence was not left in school to be thrown out as clutter; instead it was presented to Bassetlaw Museum following his death in 1995 – together with a contact address for his widow. Contact was duly made and members of the family have been pleased to offer further information.

Mr Woodward was born in Staffordshire, but completed his education at University College, Nottingham (as it was then) where he read for a London University accredited B.Sc in Geography, Geology and Botany. He played for the college cricket and football teams – and was a useful left-handed bowler. When the Second World War broke out he was teaching in Blackminster School at South Littleton near Evesham as a science specialist – so this is where the chaotic air raid practice occurred. After the war he returned there, but during the conflict he served in RAF map and signals units and saw service in Northern Ireland and India. In 1941 he married an Irish Catholic girl, Una, before being shipped out to the Far East. Eventually two of their four children were pupils at Tuxford, Veronica from 1960 to 1964 and Brian from 1962 to 1966. Both went on to become teachers themselves. When he retired Mr Woodcock continued to live in Retford until his death and he is buried in Retford Cemetery.

Former colleague Mrs Elsie Pickering recalled the character of Tuxford School's first headteacher during an interview in 2005: "Mr Woodward as a person was serious and formal in school – as most headmasters would be in those days. He stayed in his office a lot and he was a very capable administrator. In many ways he could be mistaken for a bank manager. He was a gentle, quiet man and not very forceful, but he had a clear vision of the sort of school he wished to create.

"In essence, he wished to broaden the experience of the children who were mostly living in isolated villages (and they were very isolated in those days when car ownership was uncommon). To achieve this he wanted the school to become a community of young people. Emphasis was placed on good manners, treating others with respect, dressing and behaving in a civilised manner. Community was more important than curriculum in those days – and many parents were very pleased with the safe, disciplined environment and the emphasis on manners."

To create a school based on respect and good manners Mr Woodward would clearly require as his deputy a different type of person from himself. If the mild and thoughtful

Mr Woodward and Mr Ball with Sudanese visitors.

23

Back Row: Jerry Ball, John Bee, Tom Grasby, Bernard Woodward, George Jeffcott, John Forster, Gordon Ellis, Colin Maw.
Front row: Lena Snowden, Meg Graham, Brenda Maw, Mary Wooten (School secretary), Audrey Anderson, Elsie Pickering, Pat Midworth, Shirley Rawson. Photograph taken in 1959.

administrator wished to form an effective management team around him he would need to recruit a charismatic leader of people whom he could trust to be his eyes and ears around school. Fortunately, George Albert Jeffcott – known as "Jeff" to colleagues – was perfect for the job. He was seven years younger than the headteacher but like him had served in the RAF during the war - as a pilot with Coastal Command.

Mr Jeffcott was born in South Wales in 1922 and educated in Penarth before joining the RAF. He served in Scotland and the Middle East and some of his training occurred in America and Canada. (2) When he left the service as a flight-lieutenant, in 1947, he joined the emergency teacher training scheme set up by the government in response to the shortage of teachers. After eighteen months he was fully qualified. From 1948 to 1955 he taught Geography and PE at Musters Road Secondary School, West Bridgford – for the final two years on a higher pay scale. He was then ready for more responsibility so he applied, successfully, for the Deputy Headship at Robert Thoroton Secondary School, Flintham – a temporary creation that occupied former RAF huts in Flintham Woods from 1950 to 1963. He first visited the school at Tuxford in the spring of 1958 when the main tower block was a steel skeleton. He wrote about the visit in the 1978 edition of Festina Lente, the school magazine: "I had an old van and was unable to drive it up the school drive because of all the builders' rubbish." He celebrated his 36th birthday one month before the start of term in the new school.

Elsie Pickering's lasting impression of the deputy headteacher was of a disciplinarian but she believed pupils enjoyed his control and fairness: "He was always keen on pupils making a good impression wherever they were... The morning assembly before first lesson would set the tone for the day. Jeff would ensure everyone was silent and respectful." Another early colleague, Brenda Maw, gave her assessment of his character: "He was a harder and colder character than Mr Woodward. Jeff's office was at the back of the hall in the dining

24

area. When he used the cane the boy would have to bend over against the wall and Jeff hit hard." She added that he would never fill the staff kettle and would make outrageous male chauvinist comments to stir up the ladies on the staff. Elsie Pickering certainly remembered a time when he didn't endear himself to female colleagues: "On one occasion the school was assembled in the hall prior to a visit to Eaton Hall. It was a miserable rainy day. Surveying the scene, with most of the girls wearing headscarves, he declared he was not taking out a gang of Russian peasants and they were ordered to take them off. Looking up he saw, standing at the back of the hall, all of the lady members of staff with headscarves on!"

The Woodward Jeffcott partnership was to last for twenty years. Mr Jeffcott summed up their division of responsibility – as he saw it – in a letter of June 1981: "For twenty years I worked under a headmaster who concerned himself mainly with policy and development and left all the day to day running of the school to me." (3) We have noted that Mr Woodward was "not very forceful" but did he really have little contact with staff and students? As we are considering a lengthy period of time there may be more than one answer to this question so we will certainly be returning to it later. At present we are focusing on the newly opened school and so the question was put to some of the early colleagues of the two men. Gordon Ellis who joined the staff a year after its opening stated categorically: "Mr Woodward was no walk over. He was the policy maker, he was the strategist – and Jeff was the tactician. Bernie insisted on doing the timetable, for example, even though Jeffcott would have liked to gain the experience of doing it." Elsie Pickering remembered that it was the headteacher who employed the staff and who had the more impressive academic background: "it wasn't long before the summer holiday that I learned I was to be Head of Geography and was asked to choose my textbooks. Fortunately Mr Woodward was a geographer so he could advise me on syllabuses and the timetable. I was given a budget, but I had no experience of ordering stationery etc. Mr Woodward would give me tips about teaching too, but I don't think he did any himself."

Colin Maw remembered: "In staff meetings Mr Woodward was in charge and Jeffcott sat quiet. The staff respected Bernie and they were loyal to him but they were nevertheless aware of his nervous mannerisms." Brenda Maw was certain of the head's vital input: "I would say the climate in the school that still abides to this day was created by Woodward. He would do everything that he could to maintain a good atmosphere. He was very caring… Jeff was such a strong personality and for him everything was black or white; Bernard was well attuned, in a quiet way, to the chemistry of the staff."

Mr Woodward knew that the school he was to lead was innovative, not only in building design, but also in concept. From the outset the county council envisaged that Tuxford's new school would be a specialist school – and one of a chain to be established across Nottinghamshire. A Retford Times article written just before the opening of Misterton Secondary Modern on 6 May 1957 explained that it was specifically designed for "training pupils in the pursuit and love of rural subjects" before adding "Tuxford Rural Secondary Modern… will be the equal of the Misterton School in all its aspects and wide scope." The article goes on to explain that the aim of all such schools was "to give a sound general education and to combine this with a vocational interest, particularly during the final two years of the pupils' life at school." Mr Woodward would, clearly, need to appoint well-qualified staff to form a strong Rural Studies department – but as this was one of his teaching subjects he would know what to look for in recruits. The person appointed to run the department was Jerry Ball who had graduated from Mr Woodward's old college – or university, as it was by now. – in Nottingham with a

BSc (Agric). The Maws and Gordon Ellis jointly described the school's first Head of Rural Studies as a gentle giant. "At a time when not many staff had cars he had a very posh car… He let the children wash it on Fridays, but they would let the sponge fall on the floor then wipe it on his car so it was like rubbing it with No 3 sandpaper." Jerry Ball's colleague, Pat Midworth, was remembered as "very sharp, very strict." Unfortunately she broke her nose in an accident with the pig-weighing machine just over a month after starting her first job.

Former student Peter Stead had clear memories of the two teachers: "Science (then called Rural Studies) was taught by Mr Ball and Miss Midworth. Miss Midworth was straight from college. Mr Ball was very enthusiastic, having the farm unit under his jurisdiction and obviously having much knowledge of farming. The Young Farmers' Club was run by him and was very popular. We met during the long lunch times and often had outside speakers. I became very involved in the farm unit and often volunteered (with David Smith) to go in during the holidays and look after the animals. (There was always a rota of interested pupils). We would milk the two cows and prepare the milk for collection. Feed the battery hens and collect the eggs. Feed the pigs and check the greenhouse. On one occasion when the stockman was not available we were entrusted to look after the unit entirely on our own for a weekend. Local television news did an item on the unit and as a result our photograph appeared in the Farmers' Weekly! I met up with Mr Ball again whilst at Eaton Hall. I remember asking him if he remembered a Peter Stead and a David Smith to which his reply was, 'Yes I do Peter!' He used to live in the Sutton in Ashfield area."

Tuxford County Secondary School only catered for the 11-15 age group when it opened so there were to be just 314 students in the first year. A total of fourteen staff could be recruited including Mr Woodward himself and Mr Jeffcott (who would teach PE and Maths). The Director of Education for Nottinghamshire, J. Edward Mason, writing in June 1960 to the parents of all children in the county due to transfer from a primary school that year listed the other subjects to be taught: "The aim of any secondary school is to give a good general education in English, mathematics, science, art, physical and religious education, as well as practical subjects such as homecrafts, needlework and the crafts of wood and metal." (4) Knowing that four out of five children were destined to move to a secondary modern he wished to reassure parents: "Secondary modern schools are undoubtedly the ones in which the great majority of children can best learn… The subjects taught in secondary modern schools are similar to those taken in grammar and technical schools, but they are approached in a different way and suited to the very varying abilities of the children." The absence of Modern Languages from the list of subjects suggests that this was not considered a very practical subject for less academic children.

Mr Woodward's first entry in the school log book was a list of the staff who were recruited and their subjects. The other subject conspicuously absent from the list (apart from French) is Science. It was taught via Rural Studies, not as a separate part of the curriculum. Three of the named staff had transferred with the first intake children from the elementary school in the village: Tom Grasby was the "Handcraft Specialist Teacher", Mrs Elsie Pickering was the Geography specialist who also offered English, and Miss Marjorie Marston - who was near retiring age and a temporary appointment – taught "General Form Subjects".

Colin Maw remembered that Jeffcott and Tom Grasby were like two brothers: "In the staffroom everyone had his or her own chair. Jeffcott and Grasby always sat together." Jeffcott gained a well-known nickname ("The General") soon after the school opened; his friend Grasby was "Colonel Tom". Peter Stead wrote about him in 1998: "Mr Grasby taught woodwork. He had a great influence on me. He taught me the practical skills which I still make use of today. I still have in my home the items I made – bed side cabinet, tea trolley, stool to name but three. Early this year I visited Mr Grasby at his home in East Markham. He still remembered me but sadly his health was poor. We arranged a further meeting for after Easter but unfortunately he died before we could meet again. He was able to tell me a little about some of the old staff, many of whom were still in contact with him."

Elsie Pickering continued to teach in the school until 1990 with just a brief break and for much of the time she was Deputy Head. She recalled how she came to join the staff: "I grew up in Tuxford and gained my degree and teaching qualification at Leicester. Because my mother was ill I arranged to work my long teaching practice at Tuxford Primary School. I must have done all right because the headmaster asked whether I would be interested in applying for a job there because one of the teachers was moving to another school. I said yes, so that was it. I didn't have a formal interview and I felt extremely lucky that a job near home came along just at the right time. This was about 18 months before the secondary modern opened… At some stage during my eighteen months at the primary school I learned that I would be transferring to the secondary modern with half of my class. I remember Mr Woodward, the newly appointed head, visiting me and the other staff due to transfer such as Tom. I also remember visiting the site of the new school to observe the progress of construction."

Peter Stead transferred with Marjorie Marston from the junior school. His impression of her was of someone "…very strict. She taught maths, which being one of my better subjects, meant we always got on well. I seem to think she retired whilst I was at school. I certainly remember visiting her on one occasion at her small cottage in Caunton." Gordon Ellis recalled how her teaching exasperated one parent: "One summer evening a parent travelled into Retford by bus from Elkesley to call at the Mr Woodward's house. He saw Bernie sitting inside and conducted a conversation through the open window. 'I have tried this long division and my wife has tried this long division,' he told Mr Woodward. Marjorie Marston had marked a boy's long division sum wrong several times so the father was totally bewildered and frustrated. The point is that the sum was right – the boy hadn't got it wrong at all."

Meg Graham was "Senior Mistress" meaning she was responsible for the girls' welfare and good behaviour. Her teaching subjects were Needlecraft and Mathematics. Brenda Maw remembered her as "Sister Peace! She was not a good disciplinarian in the early days because she was too gentle. She was like Bernie rather than Jeff. However, I think she hardened and learned as the years passed."

Head of English John Forster also had responsibility for the school library. Peter Stead admitted that English was not his best subject "…but I well remember many of the lessons. I can still remember class readers and poems. I remember giving a class talk entitled, 'The Railways of Tuxford'. Mr Forster may not have solved my spelling problems, but he certainly instilled the correct use of the apostrophe. In his room was the only tape recorder in the school!"

NOTTINGHAMSHIRE
COUNTY COUNCIL

EDUCATION COMMITTEE

TUXFORD
COUNTY SECONDARY
SCHOOL
(Roll: 360)

Headmaster:
B. W. Woodward, B.Sc.

MISTRESS for PHYSICAL EDUCATION. To be responsible for Girls' Physical Education and Games. Fully equipped Gymnasium and showers, changing accommodation and laundry. Excellent facilities for outdoor work, including covered games practice area, and tennis courts, hockey pitches and athletics field all on site.

MASTER or MISTRESS for MATHEMATICS. To be responsible for the organisation and teaching of Mathematics and Arithmetic and particularly for co-ordination of the work in the Craft and Rural Studies Departments.

MASTER or MISTRESS HISTORY. To be responsible for the organisation for the teaching of History through out the school and for the development of local studies in conjunction with geography and rural studies and subjects.

Applications for all posts invited from teachers who are about to leave College and for teachers with experience. In the case of a teacher with suitable qualifications and experience being appointed to of the above posts a post allowance of £90 may be available.

Application forms may be obtained from the undersigned to whom they should be returned by 23rd May, 1960.

J. EDWARD MASON,
Director of

County Hall,
West Bridgford,
Nottingham.

Deputy head, George Jeffcott and Meg Graham, senior mistress.

Audrey Anderson taught Art and Craft as well as Religious Knowledge. Apparently she could be a little clumsy and it was suggested that she broke the school pottery kiln, for example. Gordon Ellis offered an anecdote concerning her that also featured one of Mr Woodward's famous mannerisms: "Once when Lena Snowden was away Mr Woodward came into the staffroom and said, 'In fact, Mrs Snowden is away, in fact. You can in fact play can't you, Mrs Anderson?' She protested but eventually gave in and had to choose very quickly a tune for the hymn – and she chose one which really didn't fit. We struggled to fit the words to the tune - without much success."

The Girls' Homecraft teacher was J Maw – no relation to Colin and Brenda. Little is known about her unfortunately.

The History specialist was John Bee. Brenda Maw recalled that "Johnny Bee used to come in by bus and would get shaved in the staffroom – just plug in his electric razor. John Forster used to get annoyed by the shaving."

Mrs Lena Snowden ran the Music department – but, as she explained in an interview in 2005, "There was no one else to help me – and I taught every child in the school! I remember teaching classes of 40 children and having no trouble from the least of them. With no music room, I had to teach on the stage. There were two choirs, a recorder class and music theory. After asking for some three years I was sent just four brass instruments; two trumpets, a tenor horn and a euphonium. We started playing the hymns at assemblies twice a week. The other days I accompanied the hymns on the piano."

Husband and wife Colin and Brenda Maw recalled how they got their jobs at Tuxford: "We passed where the school was being built and made enquiries about working there and discovered there was a school house available in East Markham. We were working in Worcester at the time. Mr Woodward, the headteacher designate, was living in Chipping Norton and he came to visit us when the authority agreed to deploy us somewhere. We in turn visited him and got to know the family. Mr Woodward wanted to employ both of us but the authority… wanted me to work there and Colin to work at Ollerton. We refused this offer and got our way in the end." Peter Stead was taught R.E. by Mr Maw: "I enjoyed his lessons – he was good fun and his habit of arriving at the classroom with a cigarette impressed me (thank heavens I never followed the example). I remember him arriving at school with a new Skoda car and other members of staff gathering around to inspect it."

Mr Woodward and his thirteen colleagues came to the new building as pioneers. They were offering a new type of education in impressive surroundings, but they had to get used to each other and learn how to work together. Elsie Pickering recalled that they had to improvise at first: "Much of the school and grounds were unfurnished. Furniture, books, materials, paper, office equipment were not in place. My classroom at the top of the tower block had few desks and only about a dozen chairs. It also had bags of flour and large tins of jam which should have been in the kitchens." The staff could have reacted negatively to a less than smooth start, but they chose to laugh at any little problems. Brenda Maw's early impression of Tuxford School was "that it was so happy – much happier than the school I came from… The staff were all relaxed and friendly… There was a lot of teasing and joking – but there was no bitterness."

1958: 244 lunches served daily.
1975: 560 meals served.
1978: 709 meals served.

Food Glorious food....

At the new school in our induction process one of our first tasks as 4a students was to become "Table Heads" meaning that we had to set the tables up for dinner. We sat eight to a table around the perimeter of the main hall area. We had to fetch the green set of plates and tureens with the food in from the serving hatch where the meals were prepared and cooked. (Dinner times were different from what we had been used to at the primary school where we stood in a queue and were served by "Dinner Ladies" who put the food onto our plates for us). It was our task as Table Heads to ensure that the portions were fair and equal and that after the meal we allocated who was to clear up ready for the pudding. When all the tables were finished the other students were allowed out to play, but we had to clear up and wipe the table ready for the second sitting.

If we were on second sitting we had to be ready to go into school from play to set up for our dinner session. We got into trouble if we didn't notice the first sitting pupils coming out of the school, which would make us late setting up.

Extract from *Tuxford School Memories* by John Pepper.

Tuxford's First Intake:

the Social Context

Part of the first intake of students. The French Circle with Meg Graham.

Construction of Tuxford County Secondary School began in July 1957 in the same month as Prime Minister Harold Macmillan told his party that Britons "have never had it so good." Pupils arrived to begin their first term at the school on Tuesday 9 September 1958 a few weeks before the Everly Brothers topped British pop music charts with Wake up Little Susie. Life in both the school and the country was very different then from how it is in 2007, and if we are to appreciate what it was like to learn or teach in the newly-opened school we need to introduce, briefly in broad generalisation, the lost world of the late 1950s.

The Bridge on the River Kwai was one of the cinema box office successes of 1957. The film, portraying such qualities as pride, duty, stubbornness and stereotypical British eccentricity, focused on traumatic events of the past. Television programmes of the day, including Bill and Ben, Hancock's Half Hour and Dixon of Dock Green, provided a parochial view of society: all telling of petty crises affecting the humdrum lives of stock characters. In the real world, Ghana became the first Black African nation to gain independence from the UK, in March 1957, at the start of a process of changing the Empire into the Commonwealth. Britain not only had to come to terms with the war, but also had to re-adjust its position in the world. Farther afield, the Soviet Union launched the first satellite to orbit the Earth, Sputnik 1, in October 1957. The 'space race' had begun and, fleetingly, people's imaginations could soar above humdrum personal concerns to contemplate a more exciting future. In 1958 British airline BOAC launched the first transatlantic passenger jet service. In that year also Nikita

Kruschev became leader of the USSR and Charles de Gaulle became leader of France.

Older people were already worrying about the attitudes and influences of teenagers in the late 1950s: the spread of American rock and roll culture, the emerging spending power of the younger generation and the stories of anti-social behaviour on the streets. Leonard Bernstein's hit musical West Side Story, first staged on Broadway during 1957, brought gritty realism to the genre by portraying teenage gang culture in New York. In November 1957 Elvis Presley's single Jailhouse Rock was No.1 in the charts, but in the following year he was called up to serve in the US army.

Divorce was rare in Britain by modern standards before the Divorce Reform Act 1969 made the process easier and less sensational. Most children grew up with both parents living with them in family homes. Most mothers were housewives and most fathers were "bread winners" before paid maternity leave was introduced. Corporal punishment was not only tolerated in school and the home, it was regarded as the only way of disciplining unruly children. The parents of Tuxford School's first intake had served in the war, they were used to army discipline and they demanded respect and obedience from their children.

Locally, not only were there cultural, social and political differences from today, but also, the economy and infrastructure of Tuxford and district were very different then. In 1957 the area was heavily dependent on one industry, agriculture. The population density was low and many farm workers lived in tied cottages with few modern comforts. Car ownership was increasing, but not widespread so tourism had no impact except that the A1 was still the Great North Road, a single carriageway road winding through small towns including Carlton on Trent and Tuxford. The pace of life was slow in the local communities that would form the school's catchment area and that is one reason why the opening of the new school was viewed as such a significant event. It would help to break down the isolation. Former teacher Gordon Ellis speaking in 2006 recalled the fairly primitive living conditions experienced by children of the early intakes: "It is difficult to understand now, but the early children moved around the new building with awe. The laundry amazed them – where the caretaker's wife would wash their kit. Several of them still lived in homes lit by candlelight." (1) Brenda Maw, another former teacher interviewed at the same time recalled: "I can remember this little lad called David who came to school one day quite badly burned and it turned out to be a candle burn." The small numbers of children from homes with no electricity, no gas, and no indoor toilet who had little experience of life outside their hamlet would be amazed by the experience of travelling to school, mixing with so many other young people of their age and being able to light a room by the click of a switch. Far more children would be impressed by the hot air blowers in every room because central heating at home was very rare. Brenda Maw remembered: "…many of them lived in homes with outside taps and outside lavatories. It was a battle to get them to take a shower after PE because they were unfamiliar with such facilities." (1)

Brenda Maw spoke proudly of the early children attending the secondary school and of the education offered: "We couldn't enter students for GCE but we provided a good education to many bright kids who previously had not been given a chance. Before schools in those

31

days are judged, we should remember that times were very different then. We had a number of very bright children – such as Bernie's daughter – who went on to study in technical college and beyond. I remember Fred Forshaw as a bright boy of that period who went on… The average attainment on arrival was probably lower than it would be today but students would often blossom at Tuxford… The parents were so appreciative of anything that was done. The parents were astounded by the building and its facilities."

Shirley Knowles (née Fielding) was an early student at Tuxford and she confirmed that brighter children were on roll from the beginning: "I lived at East Markham and attended the primary school there before I came to Tuxford School in 1958. As changing schools drew nearer I was asked to take my eleven-plus exam. I really didn't want to go to Retford High School, which my sister was already attending. I didn't feel confident about leaving my friends and also I was excited about going to the brand new school just down the road. Another reason for not wanting to go to the high school was that I knew my parents would have to pay out for lots of equipment such as a tennis racket and books, and with my sister already attending, they probably would not be able to afford it. I passed the first part of the eleven-plus with flying colours, but when the second stage took place I conveniently had a bad stomach ache and didn't take it. I had to sit the final part of the exam on my own and I was so determined to go to Tuxford that I deliberately put a stroke through the wrong answers even though I knew most of the answers with ease.

"On my first day at Tuxford School, I walked from home via the 'cinder path' with some of my friends. As we walked up the school drive, it looked gleaming and impressive with lots of glass. Some builders were still floating around; this was quite something for the girls to talk about!" (2)

Another member of the original intake, Denise Brackenbury née Pickering, recalled her feelings on the first day: "I started Tuxford School on the very first day of its opening back in September 1958 at 13 years of age. I clearly remember walking from East Markham with several of my pals by the cinder path dressed in my grey skirt, white shirt, green blazer and a green beret. I wore this new uniform with such pride that it made me feel I had grown two feet taller." (3)

There were only 314 students in school during its first term, and fewer after the Christmas holiday as older ones left after their fifteenth birthday. Former student John Pepper wrote proudly in 2006 that he was the first student to enter the school on the first day of term: "I had a paper round which started from Newcastle Street, down Peel Avenue and onto Ash Vale where I was born and still lived at the time. Not thinking of the time (after the paper round) I quickly rode up to Tuxford, down Lincoln Road and to school. Parking my bike I rushed up the steps to find the two double entrance doors locked. Thinking I was late I banged on the doors, to be met by a bewildered Mr Jeffcott, the new Deputy Head. 'You're too early we are not ready for pupils yet,' he declared." (4)

Former teacher Mrs Elsie Pickering recalled the atmosphere in school at the start: "Lunchtime lasted about 80 minutes and both staff and students were able to enjoy their community life. Staff would play draughts or go outside for tennis. They would have time to talk and laugh together so the staff room felt very much like a social club in those days. The children could also choose from a wide range of activities. It was also the school's policy to ensure that children had a good hot meal because many travelled from so far. There was a family dining system, eight to a table, and someone went up to collect a bowl of potatoes and a bowl of vegetables etc. It was very civilised – but children would complain of the small portions that this system produced." (5)

Another kind of misgiving was recalled by former teacher Liz Bradshaw: "Although local people knew that the building design had won awards the main concern of many mothers in the village after the first intake started was the open plan stairs. The gossip suggested that boys congregated at the bottom of the stairs in the hope of catching a glimpse of thigh as girls went upstairs!" (6) Another insight into the out of lesson activities of early boys was provided by John Pepper: "The caretaker when the school opened was a Mr Hepplewhite. He was full of fun and we all got on well with him. If we older boys had chance we would go to his workshop at the back of the Laundry for a crafty cup of tea." On a more serious note Gordon Ellis suggested: "A good proportion (of the boys) felt that their working lives were mapped out for them. They expected to work on farms or in the pits."

Shirley Knowles offered a female perspective on the school's early days: "After eating our lunch we would either be in the gym with Mr. Jeffcott having jive lessons (which were brill!) or we would be with Mrs. Snowden, a lovely lady with a wonderful voice. Being in the school choir we would, as a treat, sing modern songs: one of our favourites was 'To know, know, know him, is to love, love, love him', which we would rehearse over and over again. The Christmas party was also great: a chance to wear high heels and dress to kill!" Denise Brackenbury remembered early sports competitions: "I was also in the netball and hockey teams. These were run by Mrs Maw, our gym teacher. One of my happy memories was of her husband, the history teacher and Mrs Maw coming to collect me from home on a Saturday morning by motorbike. I was delighted to be bundled into their sidecar and then we would travel to Retford, Worksop and surrounding villages to take part in netball tournaments."

John Pepper explained how much the first intake loved life in Tuxford School: "On the last day of term before the school broke up for Easter quite a few of us leavers just did not want to leave a happy and caring school that had become a big part of our lives. In fact I visited the school for a number of years after I left. I always spent the first hour with Mr Woodward, the headmaster, then after first break accompanied Mr Grasby to the woodwork room until lunch. Mr Grasby went home for lunch so I joined Mr Jeffcott for lunch. After lunch I spent the afternoon with Mr Jeffcott before heading back home to Boughton."

Naturally, the school could not retain its social club atmosphere for ever – and nor could the local area remain undeveloped in a

The new stairwell caused concern for mothers.

33

changing world. £50 million was invested in building High Marnham power station during approximately the same period as the school was being built. The station brought an influx of new workers and the need to offer them affordable homes led to housing developments in Tuxford and district. The opening of Bevercotes Colliery also stimulated house construction. Further investment was directed at upgrading local sections of the A1 to dual carriageway – bypassing towns and villages. The local aggregates industry too was given a boost by all the construction activity. New jobs and new houses brought new pupils to the school and as the school grew it inevitably changed.

The first of five generators at High Marnham power station began feeding power into the national grid on 15 October 1959. It alone could meet all the electricity demands of a city the size of Nottingham or Leicester, but when all five generators were running from 1962 Marnham was, for a short time, the biggest single station in Europe and generating twice as much electricity as Battersea power station in London.

The £6 million Doncaster / Retford by-pass was opened by Minister of Transport Ernest Marples at the end of July 1961. Amended plans for the Sutton-on-Trent, Weston and Tuxford by-pass were published in the Retford Times of 25 August 1961, but a date for construction had still to be set. For a few years more all London to Scotland traffic passed through the town.

Winding gear was being installed at Bevercotes Colliery in January 1961 and it was intended that production of coal should begin later in that year. 270 houses for workers at the pit were constructed in 1960: 86 at Elkesley, 84 at Ollerton and 100 at Ordsall. Most of these, 193 out of 270, were occupied by miners who had been transferred from Area No. 5 and their families.

Peter Stead was one of the able students who looked beyond agriculture and mining for a profession. He, like several other members of the first intake, went on to become a teacher. He recalled that the modern school was not as up to date as its title would suggest: "As I remember there was no use of television and the world of video recorders was still some distance away. We did have a radio speaker socket in most rooms to allow live BBC broadcasts to be heard. I well remember listening to the live broadcast of the first American in Space which must have been in 1962.

"At morning breaks we were supplied with our one third pint of milk in the dining area. Movement around the school was supervised by prefects. One stairway was used for movement up the building and one stairway for movement down the building. All pupils had their designated locker to keep their books in. Lockers were in corridors, but had no locks. No one would dream of interfering with another's locker.

"Pupils left school at the end of the fourth year. We took the East Notts Leaving Certificate Examination. Those who wanted to continue their education did so by going on to Worksop or Newark College of Further Education. I went on to Worksop. We were collected by coach from Tuxford each morning." (7)

The road to academic success was certainly different for early students from the smoother journey of today. However, no-one would complain about the obstacles; it was just the way that the system worked. Everything was different then.

Sources

1   *Three Early Teachers Remember*, Brenda Maw, Colin Maw, Gordon Ellis, Tuxford School Archive Papers,
      unpublished, 2006

2   *Memories of Tuxford School 1958-60* , Shirley Knowles, Tuxford School Archive Papers, unpublished, 2005

3   *Schooldays 1958-59*, Denise Brackenbury, Tuxford School Archive Papers, unpublished, 2005

4   *Tuxford School Memories,* John Pepper, School Archive Papers, unpublished, 2006

5   *Mr Woodward's School,* Elsie Pickering, Tuxford School Archive Papers, unpublished, 2005

6   *Tuxford Beginnings,* Liz Bradshaw (née Fox), Tuxford School Archive Papers, unpublished, 2005

7   *A Letter from Peter Stead*, Tuxford School Archive Papers, unpublished, 1998

Tuxford Secondary Modern School,
Notts.

10th July 1958.

Dear Parents,
May I welcome your son/daughter to the new Tuxford Secondary Modern School which will open on Tuesday 9th September, 1958, and hope that he/she will enjoy and use fully the excellent facilities which are being provided. Every encouragement will be given to your child by the members of my staff and may I ask for your support in seeing that your child attends regularly through-out the full four year course of Secondary education. It is possible that a course will extend into fifth year leading to the preparation for an exter-nal examination which will have a bearing on the future careers open to your child, and I trust that you will discuss your child's progress in relation to this with members of my staff and myself.   After the School has started, it is hoped that you will come to meetings of parents at convenient centres in the district to meet members of my staff and myself .   If you have any problems prior to the opening in September, I hope you will call and see me, write to me or telephone me at the District Education Office, Retford. (Telephone -Retford)

May I ask you to support fully the items set out below so that the start for the first term may be a smooth one .
Trusting that I shall be able to meet you personally very soon,
Yours sincerely,

BW Woodward (B.W.Woodward B.Sc.)
Headmaster.

TUXFORD SECONDARY MODERN SCHOOL - FIRST TERM COMMENCES - TUESDAY 9th SEPTEMBER.

Transport to School - Details of the picking up point will be given to your child at his/her present School.

Morning School- Starts 8.50 am. Ends 12.10.
If your child is walking or cycling to School will he/she arrive by 8.45 to avoid School Buses in the narrow School Drive

Afternoon School- Starts 1.35pm. Ends 3.50 pm.

Dinner Money should be brought on the opening day of the School week for the number of dinners required for that week.(Opening week - 4/-)

Free Meals- if your child is entitled to free meals the usual form must be obtained from his/her present School and forwarded to County Hall.

Valuables. It is not advisable for your child to bring items which may be lost or damaged during the many activities of the usual school day.
Money brought for special purposes should be handed in to the Form Teacher for safe keeping until required.

Uniform. If you are replacing clothing for your son/daughter would you please consider certain of the items from the list below . These are standard items normally worn by boys and girls and can be purchased reasonably at both,the Retford and Newark Coop. Outfitting Depts.

Boys Green Blazer and Cap (Cloth 14A or 14B). Green/Gold Diagonal Striped Tie
Grey Trousers, Shorts, Suit, Shirt, Pullover/Slipover, Socks/Stockings

Girls Green Blazer & Beret (Cloth 14A or 14 B) Green/Gold Diagonal Striped Tie.
Grey Skirt, Gym Slip, Cardigan, Stockings/Ankle Socks.
White or Cream Blouse - Plain style.

Rainwear Green Gabardine.
May I stress that I only wish you to consider these items as replacements for the future clothing of your child when your personal budget will allow this. The Managers of the Outfitting Depts at both Newark and Retford will be pleased to help you on any matter relating to School Outfitting. If there are any special problems I hope you will consult me.   The Senior Mistress(MrsGraham) who will also be our Needlework Specialist is planning to help girls design many items of Clothing as part of the Needlework scheme of work. This you will hear more of in the future when the School courses have started.

Letter to parents of the first students in July 1958.

35

On Task, On Target *The story of the first fifty years of Tuxford School*

(The following is an edited description of Tuxford School one year after it opened. Reproduced courtesy of the *Retford Times*. 21 August 1959.)

The Very Model of an Ultra-Modern School
Tuxford Experiment is Succeeding

It is always fascinating, not to say impressive, to see an ideal translated into a working reality. And as I walked round Tuxford's new Secondary Modern School, I realised that here was the dawning of a new era in the conception of education. It took Mr BW Woodward, headmaster, and myself almost three hours to walk round the school and during that time, Mr Woodward must have told me of at least 100 points where the school differs from the old-type school.

The word "link" looms largely in Mr Woodward's vocabulary and I did not have to wait long to see the reason for this. There is not one aspect of the school's teaching that is not linked, and linked strongly and directly, to matters in the outside world, and I mean the world in its widest and fullest sense. Let us take an example. There is maize growing in the sub-tropical section of the homely looking yet efficient greenhouse. Now the children see what they want to grow – corn on the cob, which of course, becomes the cornflakes on the breakfast plate. Not a new idea, home educationalists might say. No, but the manner and the thoroughness with which these things are done at Tuxford marks it out as a pioneer in this experimental field.

When I had turned off the Lincoln Road and made for the school entrance, the first thing I noticed was, on the left, the "farmyard" – yes that's right, a real live miniature farmyard. I was glad I had, because Mr Woodward explained during our walk round that that was exactly what the architect had meant to be noticed when he designed the building. The school, it must be remembered, is one with a "rural bias" and the visitor should be reminded of that first.

The husbandry section of the school's activities is in itself a miniature farm experimental station and that is no exaggeration. It is here the best ways of animal-feeding are tried out in a most scientific manner. Calves, poultry, pigs are all fed by traditional methods and new untried methods are also experimented with. The results are all carefully recorded in graph-form and comparisons made. These graphs, maths lessons in themselves, are linked with the ordinary lessons. One boy is so keen on these graphs that he does them as a hobby in his dinner hour, much to the delight and approval of the teaching staff.

Tuxford's new school was the first in the county to keep cows.

Another matter which pleases Mr. Woodward and his staff tremendously, is the fact that several of the pupils voluntarily come back to the school during the holidays and tend the crops and feed the animals. They are already learning about life at first hand. Learning much and learning fast! I met Alan Bett, head boy, twice on our walk round the school. Alan, a farmer's son from

Darlton, was trying out some new sort of harness on the noisiest of pigs – perhaps a reactionary one? - when I was first introduced. Later I saw Alan in the up-to-date school library. No, he had not chosen a farm book, it was one about cricket! I merely record this incident as being typical of the life which the children are leading at the school.

Mr Woodward showed me the fine sports field, with its running-track, jumping-pits for field events, and cricket nets and the indoor sports ground. All the children's sports clothes are washed on the school premises in what must be the world's biggest washing-machine, which looks about the size of a modern coal-house.

We went into the girls' art and craft class and the needlework room, the woodwork class and the cookery class. It seems a pity – and almost an impertinence – to dismiss all these wonderful activities in just a few, short bald sentences, but it would take a column to praise the really beautiful work turned out in these departments. But there was no need to look at the work, the confident expression on the faces of the teachers and pupils showed that they knew they were doing something worthwhile and doing it well. The children in the cookery class had been preparing a picnic and had packed it all up and were going out on to the playfield to sample their efforts. What I saw of the delicacies made me glad indeed my own dinner-time was not too far away.

From there, Mr Woodward took me to see the geography, history and mathematics classes. I rashly asked one master what he was teaching and he replied: "Revised percentages." So I hurriedly changed the subject. The teacher explained with a humanity that would not be present in the "old days" that he was of the opinion revised percentages were difficult and was taking the boys over them again to make sure they understood them. Once again a typical instance of the attitude I found among the staff.

There is a sound-proof – yes, it really is – music room which in its turn can be easily converted into a stage with its own floodlights, foot lights and arc lights. In fact all those lights so essential to the production of a successful play. In the theatre and hall combined there is seating accommodation for about 400 or so spectators, and there is a well-equipped, modern gymnasium.

It seems superfluous to say there is maximum window space in the modern manner; dusty nooks and crannies, once a seemingly inseparable part of our educational system, being noticeably absent.

A small point which impressed me was that, in spite of the modern outlook of staff and pupils, I noticed the old time standards of courtesy were not forgotten and the pupils stood up when the head entered the room.

Tuxford's Secondary School is an experiment and one that is, without a shadow of a doubt, well on the way to succeeding. But the essence of the Tuxford school, among so much that is new, is the freedom given to the individual child and also the trust reposed in them. Children are encouraged to work on their own and to use their initiative to an extent that 25 years ago might have seemed "heresy". One of the most important things Mr Woodward showed me was cupboards without locks: another way of showing the children they are trusted and very often in life if trust is given, then it will be returned. Not always, mind. But where would the human race have got to without bold experiments?

37

NEW CLOTHES

FOR THE

EMPEROR

BY
NICHOLAS
STEWART
GRAY

THURS DEC 7th
FRID DEC 8th

SETTINGS

ACT ONE

SCENE I   The Emperor's dressing room
SCENE II   Outside Auntie's cottage

TEA INTERVAL

ACT TWO

SCENE I   In the forest
SCENE II   Under the palace
SCENE III   The Emperor's dressing-room.

INTERVAL

ACT THREE

SCENE I   A workroom in the palace
SCENE II   The Emperor's dressing room.
SCENE III   Outside Auntie's cottage

Photographs courtesy of the *Newark Advertiser.*

On Task, On Target *The story of the first fifty years of Tuxford School*

Children in three-act play

Pupils of Tuxford County Secondary School gave a production of Nicholas Stewart Gray's "New Clothes for the Emperor," for their first three-act play, on the school stage, last night.

Five settings and a variety of costumes were produced by the children and staff for the production.

FIRST TIME

For many of the young players it was the first stage appearance.

Mrs. M, E. Graham and Mr. J.Foster were producers for the two-day event. Taking part were Margaret Dalley, Susan Woodward, Roger Chambers, Anne Blaine, Frederick Forshaw, Brian Home, Phillip Marshall, Brian Jackson, Michael Sheffield, Christopher Lamb. Bryan Dromfield, David Allen, and David Broughton.

Reproduced courtesy of the
Newark Advertiser, 8 Dec 1961.

CHARACTERS IN ORDER OF APPEARANCE

AUNTIE GARLYCK — Margaret Dilley
MALKYN — Susan Woodward
PRINCE RICHARD — Roger Chambers
PRINCESS DULCIS — Anne Blades
THE EMPEROR — Frederick Forshaw
THE LORD CHANCELLOR — Brian Home.
TOM PIGGOTT — Philip Marshall
EARL MARSHAL EMERY — Brian Jackson
PIERS — Michael Sheffield
PERKIN — Christopher Lamb
OTTO — Brian Dronfield
BELVEDERE — David Allen
THE JAILOR — David Broughton.
THE HM — ?

PRODUCED BY
Mrs. M. Graham.
AND
Mr. J. Forster

COSTUMES, LIGHTING, SCENERY
PROPERTIES, MAKEUP
BY
Members of staff and pupils.

TUXFORD COUNTY SECONDARY SCHOOL

Tuxford County Secondary School: The First Year

Extracts from the School Log Book for 1958-59

8th Sept. 1958

The teaching staff met prior to the opening on the 9th Sept. to check equipment, and to discuss duties and organisation. The following staff were present:-

* Mr G Jeffcott (Deputy Head) Boys' Physical Education & Mathematics.
* Mrs M Graham (Senior Mistress) Needlecraft & Mathematics.
* Mr J Forster Head of English Dept. including Library.
* Mr J Ball BSc (Agric) Head of Rural Studies Dept.
* Mr T H Grasby Handcraft Specialist Teacher.
     Mrs E Pickering BA Geography Specialist Teacher & English.
     Mr F Bee History Specialist Teacher & Gen. Form Subject.
     Mrs L Snowden F.L.C.M. Music Specialist Teacher & Gen. Form Subject.
     Mr C Maw Religious Knowledge & Remedial.
     Mrs C Maw Girls' Physical Education & Gen. Form Subject.
     Mrs J Maw Girls' Homecraft Specialist Teacher.
† Miss P Midworth Rural Studies and Rural Science.
† Miss A Anderson Religious Knowledge & Art & Craft.
Δ Miss Marston General Form Subjects.
(Mr) B W Woodward BSc (Headmaster)

> * Posts of Special Responsibility
> † Newly Qualified Teacher
> Δ Temporary Appointment

9th Sept. 1958 - The New County Secondary School, Tuxford opened at 8.50 am for its first session. The 314 pupils were allocated to 10 forms. Mid-day meals were served in the dining area to 244 pupils. A cafeteria system of dining was commenced for the first week.
  After Form business had been completed in the afternoon, the whole school assembled for its first act of corporate worship. The theme was "Pride in Craftsmanship".

15th Sept. 1958 - The "family system" of dining was introduced as the school kitchen was fully operative.

6th Oct. 1958 - Mr G Jeffcott (Deputy Head) was absent due to a severe influenzal attack.

9th Oct. 1958 - Fourth form pupils (boys) due to leave at Xmas visited a Careers Demonstration at Sir F. Milner Secondary School Retford. This was staged by the Retford Youth Employment Service in conjunction with local industry.

14th Oct. 1958 - Fire Drill Practice.

On Task, On Target *The story of the first fifty years of Tuxford School*

15th Oct. 1958 - School visited by the Director of Education, the Deputy Director, the Assistant Director and a party of over 60 County Councillors and other officials.

20th Oct. 1958 - School visited by West Riding School Meals Advisor and Miss Lawson HMI to see the school meals provision.

22nd Oct. 1958 - Miss P Midworth (Rural Science Teacher) injured with the lever action of the Pig Weighing machine.

6th Nov. 1958 - Sultan Khan (British Guiana) visited the school and talked to 3rd and 4th forms about Local Government in the Crown Colony.

17th Nov. 1958 - Demonstration to 4th Form Girls in Needlework Room of Singer Sewing Machine equipment and special attachments by Mrs N Davis (am & pm).
Pm: Visit of Physical Education HMI Mr Major to see the Physical Education facilities of the school (covered games practice area and laundry).

18th Nov. 1958 - pm. Mr P Syth (Principal of the County Farm Institute) visited the school farm unit and discussed farm financial estimates.

21st Nov. 1958 - pm. 4th form group with Mrs Graham and Mr Forster attended the dramatic performance of "The Taming of the Shrew" at Eaton Hall Training College.
pm. Mr E Shaw Drama Adviser visited the school and discussed the facilities for school Drama.

24th Nov. 1958 - Careers Evening from 6.15 to 9.30pm. All departments of the school were open to the assembly of parents. Over 200 attended, and the guest speakers were Mrs D Stringfellow, Officer of the Sheffield Hospital Board, Mr S.C Alexander B.Sc (Agric) County Farm Institute, Mr D Burnham Retford District Youth Employment Officer, Mr R.S. Clough B.Sc (Agric) The Young Farmers Club Movement. Parents were able to meet both the guest speakers and the teaching staff of the school in the second half of the evening programme.

26th Nov. 1958 - The members of the school choir (from 2A & 3A) visited the Albert Hall, Nottingham with Mr Woodward, Mrs Graham and Mrs Snowden to hear the world famous Vienna Boys choir from 7pm-9pm.

16th Dec. 1958 - 1st Year pupils in form 1A, 1B, 1C and 1S Xmas party with form teachers Miss Marston, Mrs Snowden, Mrs B Maw & Mr C Maw held during the afternoon.

17th Dec. 1958 - 3rd and 4th Year pupils Xmas party during the evening 6.30-9.30pm with members of the school teaching staff.

18th Dec. 1958 - 2nd Year pupils Xmas party during the afternoon with form teachers Mrs Pickering and Mr Bee.

19th Dec. 1958 - am. Final assembly held for the end of the first school term.

pm. Nativity play and Festival of Carols were performed under the direction of Mrs Graham, Mrs Foster and Mrs Snowden to the assembled school. The programme for the afternoon concluded with the whole school singing "Festina Lente" the school song and march accompanied by the school percussion band.

   Number of pupils on roll: 309. Number of pupils having school dinners: 242

   Number of pupils bringing sandwich meals from home: 16

8th Jan. 1959 - Mr J Ball was unable to report for duty owing to very heavy snowfall blocking roads on the Derbyshire Nottinghamshire border.

9th Jan. 1959 - The games covered practice area marked out for Basketball, Netball, Hockey, Badminton and Tennis, and pupils commenced games training in Badminton Basketball and Netball in indoor courts.

19th Jan. 1959 - Dr Nelson School Medical Officer visited the school at 9.30 to complete the Medical Inspection of pupils

21st Jan. 1959 - The Nottinghamshire secretary of the Young Farmers Club Movement (Mrs A Wathall) visited the school during the midday break and gave a talk to 128 pupils on the objects of forming a Young Farmers' Club and the aims.

22nd Jan. 1959 - Nurse Frazer visited the school and inspected the hair of all pupils. No verminous cases reported.

23rd Jan. 1959 - The chairman of the school governing body visited the school and toured all departments of the school and inspected the attendance registers.

26th Jan. 1959 - A Governors meeting was held in the staff room at 7.30pm at which the headmasters' report for the first term of the school was presented.

28th Jan. 1959 - The Carol Jewner Theatre Company presented plays both during the morning and afternoon for Junior school children from the district. Over 400 Junior children visited the school.

9th Feb. 1959 - The Rural Studies department introduced the first litter of 8 (Landrace x Large white) pigs into the farm unit.

13th Feb. 1959 - The first cases of influenza were notified and 45 pupils were absent from school.

4th Mar. 1959 - Members of Form 4 & 3 visited the egg packing station at Newark to see the eggs produced by the school poultry being tested and graded.

6th Mar. 1959 - The effect of the influenza epidemic which had been increasing daily reached its peak and 154 children were absent from school. Eight children showed symptoms after *arriving at school by bus and these were isolated as far as possible from the other pupils until they could be taken home again.*

11 Mar. 1959 - The junior and senior choirs participated in the North Lincolnshire Music and Drama Festival and junior choir were awarded a 1st Prize Certificate for their singing of "Christ is the World's True Light" theme Runkart and Crunand (Psalm 23) with descant. The choir also gained the highest marks for a set test piece and were awarded the "Lady Winifride Elwere Cup"

16th-20th Mar. 1959 - Practical tests and examinations were taken by all forms in all subjects on the curriculum and the marks were standardised and form order lists were compiled.

School Club Membership - Mar. 1959 - Young Farmers 110 Members; Chess club 50; Choirs 80; French circle 25; Badminton club 26; Dancing club 51.

Easter Vacation 26th March - 13th April 1959 - Voluntary holiday work in the Farm unit (pigs and poultry section) and in the greenhouse was carried out… Duties included feeding pigs, watering and feeding poultry collecting and recording eggs, stoking greenhouse fire, watering plants and seeds and opening ventilation in greenhouse. Cleaning out pigs and bedding down. Weighing pigs. Cleaning out poultry. Packing eggs for despatching.

13th Apr. 1959 - Summer Term commenced.

14th Apr. 1959 - School visited by Mr Jones (Assistant Director) Mr A Goodman (Architect Dept) Mr P Lyton (Farm Institute) Mr Batchelor (Playing Fields) for site extension meeting a 11.am.

15th Apr. 1959 - Mr Davies and Miss Brogden physical education advisers for Glamorgan visited the school to see the Physical Education Facilities.

18th Apr. 1959 - The Director of Education (J Edward Mason MA MEd) and Mrs Mason and Sir Edward Herbert High Sheriff and Lady Herbert visited the school at 3.30 and stayed until 6pm seeing the range of modern school buildings and provision in each department at Tuxford

22nd Apr. 1959 - 12+ examination papers received at the school. Mr J. Forster appointed to i/c examination with other staff invigilators for the 28th April 1959 9.30-3.00pm.

28th Apr. 1959 - 12+ examination taken by Janet Moody 1A.

28th Apr. 1959 - Meeting held at the school to discuss the secondary modern school brief. The Assistant Director (Mr Jones), the County Architect's representatives, Education advisory staff and Head teachers (18) were present at 10.30am. The meeting terminated at 4pm

29th Apr. 1959 - School visited by the Chairman of Governors Mr S S Housley and Mrs Housley and other members of the governing body with their wives. All departments of the school were visited and pupils were watched in various activities. At the termination of the afternoon session the Governors and their wives were entertained to tea in the staff room.

15th May 1959 - *A sheep shearing demonstration for all 3rd and 4th year pupils was held in the school farm yard. Mr Featherstone from the county farm institute demonstrated the New Zealand sheep shearing method and the British traditional method. Sheep for shearing were loaned by Mr S S Housley (Chairman of Governors).*

20th May 1959 - *Mr Bee, Mrs Pickering and Miss Anderson visited the Museum at York to see the period settings with form 3A as part of their Social Studies curriculum.*

1st June 1959 - *34 pupils reported to the Tuxford clinic for polio injections.*

5th June 1959 - *Visit to the school of the Director of Education and the conference of Grammar School and Technical School Headmasters (22 county headteachers).*

11th June 1959 - *Members of the Nottinghamshire Rural Studies Association; the Director of Education, the Chairman of Governors and the Headmaster of the Primary School (Mr W R Blackwell) were entertained for lunch and tea; and during the afternoon toured the School and particularly the Rural Studies facilities and developments.*

12th June 1959 - *Governors' Meeting in the Staff Room at 8.00pm to interview candidates for the post of Stockman, Gardener, Groundsman. The post was offered to Mr C Stanniland and was accepted.*

23rd June 1959 - *The School 1st XI cricket and 1st VI chess teams were entertained at the Grove School, Balderton to matches. The home side were victorious in both events. Folk dancing instruction was introduced into the curriculum.*

25th June 1959 - *Interviews were held for the post of Assistant Caretaker at 8.00pm in the Staff Room. The post was offered to Mr H N Wiggett and was accepted.*

29th June 1959 - *Miss B A Eastgate (Homecrafts Teacher) commenced duties in the School on a part-time basis.*

2nd July 1959 - *A special demonstration of electrical appliances (spin driers and the use of the grill boiler) took place in the Homecraft Room. This was given by Miss Flowers, demonstrator for the Electricity Board to girls of Form 4A, 4B and 3G.*

11th July 1959 - *The High Sheriff of Nottinghamshire (Sir Edward Herbert) at the invitation of the Nottinghamshire County Council Education Committee held a Garden Party at the School at 3.00 pm in order to allow the visitors from all spheres of life to see one of the superb Schools which the Authority were erecting in the County.*

14th July 1959 - *The Commonwealth Education Conference Study Tour 'C' comprised of the following members: Mr J Bunting, Chief Federal Advisor on Education – Nigeria, Mr P*

Donohue, Assistant Director of Education – Hong Kong, Dr H L Haslegrave, Principal of Loughborough College of Technology, Mr W C Little, Secretary to the Ministry of African Education, N Rhodesia, Mr Mohamed Yusoff, Leader of the Malayan Federation – Federation of Malaya, Dr N K Sidhanta, Vice Chancellor, Calcutta University – India, Mr C M Obuobisa Mate, Leading the Ghanian Delegation – Ghana, Mr Abdulla Ibrahim Saidi, Member in charge of the Education Department – Aden, Mr J S Brunton, Senior Chief Inspector for Schools for Scotland – UK, Mr K G Wilson, Director of Studies, Madrid – British Council, Mr R A Hack Regional Director, Ibadan Nigeria - British Council, together with the Assistant Director of Education for Nottinghamshire (Mr Jones) the chairman of the Education Committee (Alderman Thompson) the Vice Chairman of the Education Committee (Mr Pugh) and Mr Swain of the county architect's department met in the school and later toured the school and were entertained for tea.

16th July 1959 - THE OFFICIAL OPENING OF TUXFORD COUNTY SECONDARY SCHOOL AT 3pm

21st July 1959
The first Annual School Sports were held in the afternoon and both parents and members of the Governing body were present. The teams from each House competed for a Sports Cup donated by Mr & Mrs G H Sutton and St Oswald House were placed first at the end of all the events. Mrs Sutton presented the Cup to the boy and girl Captains of the winning House. 41 standards were reached during the afternoon.
   Results: St Oswalds House - 91 points; St Lawrence House - 86 points; St Peters House 81 points; St Nicholas House - 81 points

23rd July 1959
The whole school was assembled in the presence of the Chairman of the Governing body Mr S S Housley. A review was given by the Headmaster of the main events of the year which were landmarks in the development of the school as a community…
   The results of the House Effort Championship:-
   1ST St Lawrence House (456 effort marks); 2ND St Peters - 384; 3RD St Nicholas - 367; 4TH St Oswald 303
The championship trophy donated by Mr S S Housley was presented to the captain of the St Lawrence house.
11am Members of form 3A & 2A under the direction of Mrs Graham produced the play "The Princess and the Woodcutter" and the members of the French Circle sang a selection of French songs to the assembled school.

23rd July 1959
Headmaster's tea for staff 3pm.

27th July to 31st July 1959
A residential course for secondary school pupils at the County Farm Institute, Brackenhurst was attended by three pupils from the school, Brenda Witts 4B, Richard Elvidge 4A, Enid Billington 3A.

Corporal Punishment in the First Term

Number Of Offenders	Offence	Punishment	Punishment Administered By
2	Unruly behaviour on stairs	1 stroke of cane	Mr Jeffcott
3	Disobedience – playing on heap of soil during lunch	1 stroke of cane	Mr Jeffcott
1	Bullying of girl	2 strokes of cane	Mr Jeffcott
1	Destruction of school fitting	2 strokes of cane	Mr Woodward
3	Unruly behaviour on school bus	2 strokes of cane	Mr Woodward
2	Throwing dirt on woodwork and disobeying prefect	1 stroke of cane	Mr Jeffcott
1	Dangerous behaviour on stairs	2 strokes of cane	Mr Woodward
5	Defying prefect when sent outside	1 stroke of cane	Mr Jeffcott
3	Running on grass after repeated warnings	1 stroke of cane	Mr Jeffcott
2	Throwing toilet paper about the cloakroom	1 stroke of cane	Mr Jeffcott

Extract from *Tremor No. 4*, Tuxford School Magazine April 1984.

Intrepid reporter Vicki Hill tracked down the man who, all that time ago, had the privilege of being FIRST – yes, FIRST folks, in the punishment book of the new Tuxford School. His name: Robert Fox. This is HIS story.

"I will always remember standing on the steps of the new school on the first day it opened its doors, for not only was it a new building, but for a lot of us a different way of being taught at a time when not only schools but a lot of the world was changing and learning at a rate never seen before…

"It all started with Mr Jeffcott a few days after starting the school. Before going to upstairs classrooms we queued up outside the rear entrance and then filed inside in an orderly fashion. Having gone a few steps up the stairs I heard this booming voice saying, 'Come here boy!' Somehow because of the beady eyes peering at me through the stairs , I knew I was the boy being referred to. 'Me, Sir?' I said. 'Yes, you boy.' This is where the plot thickens and my second mistake was to turn and walk down the same stairs. Silly boy, I should have known after two or three days that you didn't walk down the same set of stairs, and so rule number two was broken.

After establishing that I had committed a crime, an example had to be set and so I had to report to the Head's study at the appointed time. I was told what I had done wrong, which was talking on the stairs. I received the cane for the first time in my life and if I remember correctly it was the first time punishment had been given in the school. I must admit I felt hard done to at the time."

My Term as Head Boy, Autumn 1958

By Ivor Nettleton

My first experience of the new Tuxford County Secondary School was in the summer holidays (August) 1958 when I volunteered to assist the then woodwork teacher Mr Grasby in moving the woodwork benches and tools from our old school, Tuxford Elementary School, and setting them up in the new school on Landa Grove ready for its opening. It all appeared very grand. Taking the benches from a 1930s army barracks style wooden hut into a ultra modern workshop with all new machinery was like a dream.

While I was there it gave me the chance to have a look around. The size was overwhelming. You could have fitted all four classrooms of the old school into the secondary school's assembly hall. At the front of the hall was the sort of stage that I had only seen previously in a theatre. On my tour I came across rows of lockers. "What are they for?" I enquired. Having only ever kept books in my desk this was all a new experience.

I met the new headmaster Mr Woodward, but not for the first time as I had been introduced to him previously as a new member of the Tuxford Tennis Club - at which time his employment was unknown to me!

After looking round, there were further tasks to do such as setting out desks and chairs for other teachers whose names now escape me. Other pupils were there to help too.

Tuesday 9th September 1958 was the start of the first term at the new school (and the last for me). My memory is a little vague as to who went to which form all those years ago, but I was in 4A with Mr Jeffcott located behind the stage. We were amazed that most subjects were taught in dedicated classrooms because previously, in our old school, we had been in one classroom all day for all subjects. In our first week there was a lot of confusion, especially on the stairways, as we tried to find the right classroom for the next lesson. As the school was new every one was guessing - even some teachers - which subject was taught in a particular room.

It was decided to have prefects in the school and I found myself appointed as one of them. In fact I was named as head boy for which office I received a badge saying "CAPTAIN' (this being the only one available at the time). Duties included reporting to the teachers anyone breaking the rules, one of which was that everyone must be out in the play area at break times. This rule caused us the most problems for the toilets were now inside, whereas in the old school the toilets were outside - in a freezing brick outbuilding. For some children indoor flush toilets were luxurious as in Tuxford and other villages they were relatively new then.

We were used to everyone having free milk provided at morning break, but now a school tuck shop was available for purchasing biscuits. Lunch time brought another new routine. Dinners were served in tureens to tables of possibly four pupils so they could be shared; often this allowed us to have more of what we liked than previously in the old school where ready plated dinners were placed in front of us.

Christmas came very quickly that year leaving me wishing that more of my school time had been spent in the new school.

National Policy and Local Regulation

Two key decisions at the start of Tuxford School's history were taken at local government level: to open a secondary modern rather than a comprehensive at Tuxford in 1958 and to designate it as a rural school. Both had a profound effect during the school's early years upon building design, the equipment purchased and the staffing structure. Both decisions were ultimately overturned, but for twenty years the LEA enforced its original vision for the school - although, as the years passed, the farm unit was reputedly denied sufficient funding to keep up with developments in agriculture. One senior member of staff at Tuxford in the 1970s suggested, off the record, that children from farming families had much more advanced equipment at home by that period than the unit could offer.

Another aspect of local regulation was that county decided which courses and examinations were offered in schools – but there is evidence that maverick headteachers resisted LEA constraints. A Retford Times article of 10 June 1960 records the extraordinary story of how secondary modern children in the county were denied the opportunity to take GCE O' level examinations – even though similar children in other parts of the country could take them. The issue had first been discussed in 1952 when teacher representatives had apparently expressed reservations about any proposal that would "enslave" secondary moderns to an external examination system. Nevertheless, two secondary modern schools, Carlton Cavendish and Bramcote Hills, had sought Education Committee approval in 1955 and 1956 respectively to offer O' level courses and the committee became aware that six other secondary moderns had begun such courses without seeking approval. As support for O' level had been demonstrated, it is surprising that a few months later, in May 1957, a conference attended by all headteachers of county secondary modern schools concluded that a county or regional exam was preferable because O' level would place "heavy demands on the most able members of the staff with inevitable damage to the rest of the school." There was some substance to this argument at the time because we should remember that the school leaving age was 15 then. Two year O' level courses would indeed tie up staff and resources. During 1958 and 1959 secondary schools in the north of the county, including Tuxford, banded together with Worksop Technical College (later North Notts F.E. College) to introduce examinations leading to a local Leaving Certificate and a similar group formed another consortium in the south of the county. The LEA characterised this co-ordinated development, unconvincingly, as "spontaneous movements by the secondary modern schools" and used this as justification for discouraging preparation for O' level. In November 1959 Nottinghamshire County Council endorsed an Education Committee recommendation to introduce the ban. (1) At the same time the transfer of late developers

Duke of Edinburgh award participants in 1963.

The official certificates.

to grammar schools was made easier – on the recommendation of the headteacher rather than by sitting an examination.

Ironically, secondary modern schools within the county found themselves admitting students into the fifth year shortly after the county ruling – and before the raising of the leaving age. A new national qualification was introduced in 1965, the Certificate of Secondary Education (or CSE). A CSE grade 1 was supposed to be the equivalent of an O' level pass – but without the prestige. The certificates were awarded by fourteen regional bodies, but the exam was promoted at government level. Tuxford headteacher Bernard Woodward had not been involved in the debate over the introduction of O' level as he was appointed after the headteachers' conference mentioned above, and now he had no choice but to accept CSE even though the same arguments could be applied against it: it too tied up resources for the benefit of a few. Mysteriously, he made no mention of CSE when he reported during the 1966 Speech Day that 17 students had stayed on for a fifth year during 1965/66 and that 14 of these had completed their courses. (2) At the start of the academic year the school log book records that senior management had not only taken the decision to allow fifth year students to be prefects (which presumably would not have pleased some of the fourth year hopefuls) but also to give more hours of employment to Mrs Elsie Pickering, one of the original teachers now returning after having a family, to assume responsibility for "Optional Studies of 5th Year CSE pupils". The introduction of CSE caused some controversy in the Tuxford staffroom. Several former colleagues remembered one lady refusing to teach the CSE syllabus, saying that she did not wish to be restricted by exam requirements.

Another national initiative of 1965 was the publication of Circular 10/65 by Secretary of

State for Education Anthony Crosland. In this he requested that LEAs reorganise all selective secondary schools into comprehensives taking the full ability range. Some LEAs responded quickly to the requested change – many of them Conservative controlled. Nottinghamshire already had comprehensives and it was in no hurry to make sweeping changes, preferring to phase in reorganisation area by area. It was the turn of Tuxford in 1976 – a year after Newark and before Retford. This is discussed in detail in later sections, but reorganisation was another milestone in the school's history and both local and national policy-makers had taken the necessary decisions. (In the mid 1960s it was envisaged that the re-organised Tuxford School would have no sixth form, but would cater for the 11-16 age group. Mr Woodward, addressing parents attending the 1966 Speech Day, expressed his concerns about the lack of educational provision for 16+ students and this may have influenced the LEA decision to reconsider plans for a sixth form at Tuxford).

The process of reorganising the school in 1976 was controlled by county. Another new teaching block was built – although it was not ready on time. Mr Woodward was given leave of absence to plan timetables, curriculum and staff appointments, but there is little doubt that the two big ideas to be implemented as part of the process were county's, not his: creation of a semi-autonomous Lower School Unit and the grouping of all teaching staff into four faculties. Both proposals were consistent with the county strategy of establishing smaller units inside comprehensives so that students would feel more at home rather than overwhelmed and alienated. (In earlier comprehensives the units had been houses). Unfortunately implementation of the staff structure turned into a public relations disaster – so, ironically, it was the staff who felt alienated. Acting Headteacher George Jeffcott recorded in the school log book that there was staff resentment following rejection of all internal candidates for the four Director of Faculty posts – not a good start to reorganisation. (3) At least two heads of department felt that they had been led to believe that they would be appointed to the new faculty roles. They never overcame their resentment and bitterness.

The raising of the school leaving age to 16 had been a principle of national education policy from the 1944 Education Act onwards. However, the date of implementation was repeatedly postponed until it was finally introduced at the beginning of the 1972/73 academic year. Unfortunately, the short term impact on Tuxford School was adverse because whilst the new teaching block provided by county improved art, craft and mathematics teaching accommodation it did not address the inadequate number of general classrooms for all other subjects. Peggy Granger recalled that classes at that time were sometimes taught on the landings in the original "tower" block because no rooms were available. (4)

Parents in Harby and North Clifton battled with the county council during

The *first* John Perry to work for the school 1964-68.

1972 to continue sending their children to Collingham Woodhill Secondary School instead of to Tuxford. They were concerned about longer travelling times and reduced opportunities to attend after-school activities. A meeting at Harby was convened in April so the Director of Education, James A. Stone could explain that Collingham Woodhill was due to be phased out. The Retford Times reported that the parents were persuaded to accept the decision. (5)

So far we have focused on national and county initiatives which had a major impact on life in Tuxford School, but there were routine regulations and influences too that would restrict Mr Woodward's freedom to manage. As a "controlled school" Mr Woodward's school received its funding from county and it was obliged to use county services to spend it. Staff vacancies were advertised via the area education office, the area education officer attended interviews and contracts were issued by county hall via the area education office.

Gordon Ellis and Ron Hardwick lead Derbyshire trip 1963.

Payroll services paid salaries, county contractors ran the school meals service and kept the school building and grounds tidy, county inspectors maintained standards in classrooms through observation and discussion. Nevertheless it was the headteacher and his team who established the learning environment in the school. It is obvious but still worth recording that Tuxford teachers decided what happened in individual lessons. The headteacher decided whether there would be a school uniform and he set the rules.

National politicians (assisted by civil servants) introduced secondary education for all after 1944. Local councillors (advised by local education authority staff) decided that one of the secondary schools should be in Tuxford and that it should be a specialist rural school. Strategic educational decisions such as these were taken then – and continue to be taken now – at national and county level because educational standards need to be high for all, not just for the lucky few, and each generation of school children has a right to equal opportunities. However the imposition of identical regulations in several schools does not result in identical schools; there is and always has been plenty of scope for interpretation.

Sources

1   *External Examinations in Secondary Modern Schools*, Retford Times, 10 June 1960

2   *Tuxford school to be extended to rural all-in*, Newark Advertiser, 20 November 1966

3   *Entry for 26 January 1976*, Tuxford School Log Book 1972-80, County Archives

4   *Looking Back*, Peggy Granger, Tuxford School Archive Papers, unpublished, 2007

5   *Parents concede in move battle*, Retford Times, 14 April 1972

Tuxford's new school has its own farm

TUXFORD County Secondary School, officially opened on Thursday, can claim to be the first built on the county's new "rock 'n' roll" system, the first with an open-air gymnasium - and the first to keep cows.

The school has been planned with a rural bias and includes a farm, greenhouse, garden room and rural science laboratories. Through this method the children are taught not only rural subjects which will be useful to them in a rural life but the broader education subjects.

"The children have been told they had failed an examination and having failed they tend to give up. But we have to develop their mathematical and English and other abilities - we have to tackle it from another angle," the headmaster, Mr. B. W. Woodward, told the "Advertiser."

Reproduced courtesy of the *Newark Advertiser.* 16 July 1959.

School Farm

The farm at the school includes pigs, brooders, chickens, and two calves - it will eventually have two milking cows - and has a stock of an approximate value of £140.

"Any profit which is made goes straight to the education authority but the main idea is to teach through the farm, not to make a profit," the man in charge of the rural science department, Mr. J. G. Ball, told the "Advertiser".

Mr. Ball has a degree in agriculture from Nottingham University, a teaching diploma and considerable practical farming experience.

The farm is paying dividends among the pupils. It has to be staffed throughout the year and there is no lack of volunteers to work during the school holiday periods. And the school has the largest Young Farmers' Club in the county with 110 members.

Reproduced courtesy of the *Newark Advertiser.* 16 July 1959.

The 1973* and 1977 Buildings
Pressures of space and curriculum

The 1958 building was designed for a student population of 360. In the first year just 314 students enrolled, but a job advert of May 1960 revealed that school numbers had already reached 360 in that year. In the following September there were 391 and Mr Woodward told parents attending the July 1961 Speech Day that numbers were expected to rise to "well over 400" in the autumn. Clearly Tuxford School had inadequate accommodation for the numbers attending from the start but, to be fair, extensions had been envisaged before the original building opened because some curriculum areas were poorly served. Music, one of the strongest and most successful subjects of the early years of the school, had to be taught on the stage in the hall because there was no specialist room. There was no metalwork shop, no science accommodation other than rural science and planners believed that at least one additional general classroom (for history and geography) was needed.

Early view of housecraft room - before the RoSLA block was built.

The RoSLA (Trent) building.

The 1956 architect's drawing shows the proposed location of the planned rooms. The music / rehearsal room was to be located at the rear of the amphitheatre: further forward than the library (later the drama studio) that eventually stood on roughly the same east-west alignment. A new corridor would be built in line with the rear of this music room to connect an extension of the gym to an extension of the housecraft / cookery room, i.e. effectively enclosing the amphitheatre courtyard. Off this corridor – set back from the music room and next to the sports "barn" – would be the additional humanities room and the science room. The new metalwork extension was planned for the space behind the woodwork and art rooms (better known to most former students as Science 1 and Science 2 respectively).

The Newark Advertiser of 9 August 1961 revealed the county education committee's minor works for the year. Among the schemes listed was an allocation of £12,000 to create metalwork, technical drawing and domestic economy rooms at Tuxford County Secondary School. However, headteacher Bernard Woodward made no mention of this development when speaking to parents attending the Speech Day in July. Instead he was encouraging parents to let their children complete a full four year course rather than allowing them to leave as soon as they were able, i.e. at the end of the term during which they celebrated their fifteenth birthdays. He was pleased that many were indeed opting to stay on. (1)

The proposal to build new craft rooms was carried forward to a revised spending programme after project funding for the county was cut by the Ministry of Education (from £235,000 for 1961-2 and £255,000 for 1962-3 to £165,000 over the two years). Work was due to start on the ten remaining projects by 31 March 1963, but for some reason the work was shelved again.

Addressing the 1966 Speech Day in November Mr Woodward was still looking forward to promised extensions, but there was more urgency now as the school leaving age was due to be raised to 16 in 1971 and plans to turn the school into an 11-16 comprehensive were being discussed. The school leaving age decision had been announced by the government in 1964 and the comprehensive move was instigated by DfES Circular 10/65 issued in July 1965. Mr Woodward revealed on Speech Day 1966 that he already had a fledgling fifth year in the school: seventeen students had opted to stay on during 1965/66 when the CSE (Certificate of Secondary Education) was introduced as a new national qualification, of whom fourteen completed the year. The new building was now in the 1969/70 building programme. (2)

There was yet another delay before New Block was eventually constructed during 1972/73 to provide places for another 120 students. Kitchen extensions and the new library block (mentioned above) were built at the same time. In the school's official log book at the beginning of September 1972 Mr Woodward commented on the "slow progress of work" and it was not until 14th June 1973 that a hand over meeting was arranged. New Block, subsequently known as the RoSLA Block and then the Trent Building provided rooms for the subjects already identified: music, metalwork, technical drawing and housecraft / home economics. In addition it became the base for mathematics and art. It was a single storey construction within the grounds of the farm unit and at a slightly lower level than the original 1958 block. Approximately half of the block was given over to craft rooms each with external doors exiting onto the farm unit track connecting cowshed to field. The other half of the block had standard classrooms connected by a narrow corridor. Like the main building, the block was not always a comfortable place to work in: it was baking hot in summer and freezing cold in winter and little thought had been given to the inappropriate juxtaposition of a music practice room along the corridor from maths rooms. The corridor was narrow too so it caused congestion and jostling at lesson changeover.

In September 1972 there were 397 students on roll, almost the same as in 1961, so the pressure on space had not grown as quickly as feared at one point. However, 1972 was the revised implementation date for raising the school leaving age and so the fourth year students would be the first cohort to remain in school for an additional

Reproduced courtesy of the *Newark Advertiser*. 15 July 1972.

New intake for Tuxford school

Notts Education Committee has reaffirmed its previous decision that children from Harby and North Clifton primary schools should in future transfer to Tuxford Secondary School instead of Collingham.

The committee had reconsidered the proposals after the matter had been referred back to them by the county council.

A £187,000 240-place extension for the Tuxford school has been included by the Department of Education and Science in a preliminary list of projects for a start in 1975-76.

55

year. Consequently, in the following September there were 498 on roll – so, once again, the school was full immediately after construction was completed. In fact it had already exceeded its designed capacity. A few additional students from the east bank of the River Trent were included in the number – but only after parents in Harby and North Clifton lost their battle with the county council to continue sending their children to Collingham Woodhill Secondary School. They had argued that the change would involve considerably longer travelling time for their children and reduce their opportunities to attend after-school activities. Parents had been informed of the decision in January 1972, but protests followed and so the Director of Education, James A. Stone, and the chairman of the Education Committee, Ald. Fred Rudder, visited Harby School in April to speak to parents. The visitors explained that Collingham Woodhill was due to be phased out. The Retford Times account of the meeting reported that "After more than an hour of searching questions the meeting was closed by Harby School headmaster, Mr K. Blythe. The parents had, reluctantly, conceded victory." (3)

Mr Woodward was pleased that the new art and woodwork areas would free the existing rooms in the original building for conversion. They became science rooms. Roger Longden who joined the staff in January 1972 as the school's new science teacher (and went on to become head of a large science faculty then, later, assistant headteacher) recalled his arrival during a 2006 interview: "The only science room was for teaching rural science. There was no physics, no chemistry, no biology as such, but general science was on the curriculum. It was a requirement of the raising of the school leaving age that a full science syllabus had to be introduced so I was appointed to teach it. John Parker joined me in September 1973 and then as a subject area we did not expand again until the school went comprehensive... A new "RoSLA" teaching block opened in September 1973 and its designed use indicates the prevailing education policy. It was to be a craft block." (4) The 1950s local education authority policy to create a string of rural secondary schools across the county, each with attached farm units, did not appear quite so far-sighted in the 1970s. The decline in agriculture had not been foreseen. Capital and staff resources tied up in farm units – if they could have been diverted – might have enabled schools to respond more quickly to an increasing need for engineering and scientific skills.

The new library near the sports "barn" freed up its former home on the ground floor of the "tower block". Briefly the latter became a staff room and then the sixth form common room. Little imagination went into the design of the 1973 library; it was only a bigger than usual single classroom. It had a flat roof and its external walls were clad in concrete panels as were those of the worst type of 1960s flats - and it suffered similarly from condensation.

Before the RoSLA and library blocks opened another extension of Tuxford School was already being planned. The Newark Advertiser of 28 July 1973 reported that 240 additional places were to be provided at a cost of £215,475. This was a county response to national education policy: after the 1964 general election the Labour government "requested" Local Education Authorities (LEAs) in England and Wales to begin converting their secondary schools to the comprehensive system. In practice, the DfES used its financial muscle to make opposition difficult by refusing to fund any new secondary school which was not a comprehensive. (A number of LEAs supporting the selection system, such as Bromley and Surrey, found it necessary to go comprehensive). However a Conservative government was returned in June 1970. The new education minister, Margaret Thatcher, withdrew the Circular and allowed each authority to decide its own policy; Nottinghamshire continued with plans to convert to comprehensives.

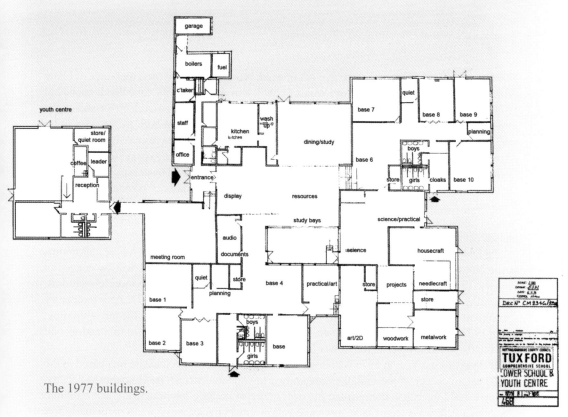

The 1977 buildings.

The Retford Times of 3 January 1975 reported that the Tuxford School would be reorganised in 1976 as an 11-18 comprehensive. It is interesting to note how quickly the estimated building cost had risen because it was reported to be "£282,000 at June 1974 prices." Another interesting aspect to the proposal was that the building of another future extension was envisaged: "Ultimately further building will be needed for the Sixth Form and it is intended that this should be provided as and when viable Sixth Form numbers come through". (5) This third major extension / building was never provided. The site for the new "Lower School" block was to the west of the original 1958 building.

Headteacher Bernard Woodward is unlikely to have influenced the decision to create a separate unit for younger students in the school. Part of the local education authority response to changing to comprehensives was the provision of small self-contained units in them, when appropriate, to provide children with the best possible start to secondary education. The units enabled younger pupils to get to know each other and secondary school teaching methods in a safe small-scale environment away from the distractions of rougher older children and long treks between lessons. Dick Fursey, who took up post as Co-ordinator of Lower School Studies and

The Lower School (Clumber) block.

On Task, On Target *The story of the first fifty years of Tuxford School*

Welfare at Tuxford one term before the unit opened, brought with him the experience of being deputy head of a similar unit at South Wolds School, Keyworth from the time that it opened in 1971. The Keyworth unit had opened when South Wolds became a comprehensive and so the same opportunity arose when Tuxford changed status. The designs of both were very similar too: an open plan building comprising teaching "bases" around a large resource area.

Tuxford County Secondary School ceased to exist at the end of August 1976 and Tuxford Comprehensive School was born. The Lower School extension could have been ready in time for the first comprehensive intake because the change of status had been planned many years in advance, but only five classrooms were ready at the start of the new term. The information booklet given to parents of the first comprehensive intake prior to transfer gives details of the phased occupation programme:

"The Lower School Unit will not be fully operational until September 1977. Five classrooms in the building will be ready for September 1976. The Craft/Science area will be opened in January 1977 and the remainder which includes the Resource Area, five more classrooms, the Dining Area and the Administration block will open in September 1977. As a temporary measure in 1976/77 first year children will receive some of their lessons in the main building, but in 1977 with the exception of Music, P.E. and Rural Studies all lessons for first and second year pupils will take place in the Lower School Unit." (6)

The Head of First Year in 1976 was English teacher Peggy Granger and she was based in the south eastern corner of the unit, the area known to later students as the Humanities Faculty. During a 2007 interview she recalled the experience of moving into an incomplete building: "No proper walkways were made, just some yellow gravel tracks, and it was a particularly wet autumn. There was no heating until gradually they introduced portable stoves. The children were coming in with their shoes absolutely covered in mud and I was bringing newspapers from home to put down in the entrance. It was appalling. On the last morning of term I took children to Tuxford Church to practice for the carol service later in the day, but had to go back there in the dinner hour to clean it." (7)

The information booklet published in 1977 for the next intake described the building: "The Lower School Unit has been built to suit the needs of children in the 11 – 13 age range and incorporates features of both primary and secondary schools in its design." Two groups of five classrooms were situated at diagonally opposite ends of the building. Wing Area North was for first year pupils in 1977 and Wing Area South was for second year pupils. The resource area was in the middle (known as the Partnership Room after a refurbishment in 1995). (8) The classrooms were called bases and one in each wing was open plan in design, i.e. not fully enclosed by walls and with no door: B5 in the south eastern wing and B10 in the north west. Craft rooms occupied the south of the building and science was between these and the resource area. A dining room was next to the resource area on the east and a "meeting room" was north-facing. The information booklet explains the role of the meeting room: "This has been designed as a multi-purpose room and will be used for year assemblies, lead lessons, lectures, discussions, drama and some music. It will also be used for film and T.V. viewing as immediately to the rear is an audio visual aids room staffed by a full time technician."

The single storey 1977 building was more compatible in appearance with the original 1958 school than the stark RoSLA block. Attractively clad in red tiles, it occupied a pleasant position on high ground above a lawn that gently sloped down to the bus park. There was a lawn to the west too and at the rear of the building were tennis courts. On the inside the building was well-provided with toilets, storage and office spaces. The classrooms were adequate in size

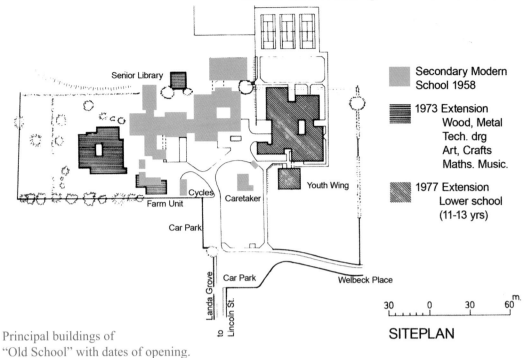

Principal buildings of
"Old School" with dates of opening.

for classes of less than thirty young people aged thirteen or under. The small scale had been a design principle which was effective so long as the use remained the same. When, first through pressure on space then to provide each teaching faculty with a permanent base, the school decided to timetable lessons for older students in the building it became obvious to everyone that the rooms were small and inconvenient. Several internal alterations were made over the years but most of the rooms were never adequate for their changed role.

Mr Woodward retired as headteacher in 1978. During his time as head the school population had grown from 314 to almost 800 and the teaching accommodation had increased from one building to three. The school was thriving and expanding – and Mr Woodcock could leave confident that a sixth form block would be provided by county at some time in the future as promised.

*   Different dates are given in some printed sources as years when construction started are cited.
Here the completion dates are preferred.

Sources

1   *Tuxford School Prize Day*, Retford Times, 4 August 1961

2   *Tuxford School to be extended to rural all-in,* Newark Advertiser, 20 November 1966

3   *Parents concede in move battle*, Retford Times, 14 April 1972

4   *My Early Days at Tuxford*, Roger Longden, Tuxford School Archive Papers, reproduced below, 2006

5   *Plans for Comprehensive Education: Tuxford and Retford and North East*, Retford Times, 3 January 1975

6   *Information Booklet September 1976*, Tuxford School publication, June 1976

7   *Looking Back,* Peggy Granger, Tuxford School Archive Papers, unpublished, 2007

8   *Information Booklet September 1977*, Tuxford School publication, June 1977

Tuxford County Secondary School
Extracts from the School Log Book for 1972-73

(Note: The New Block mentioned in the entries below was subsequently known as 1. the RoSLA Block and 2. the Trent Building; the new Library block, built at the same time, later became the Drama Studio).

4th Sept. 1972
397 on roll. Two more feeder schools allocated, Harby and North Clifton.
Mr Brook, Secondary School Adviser, called during the afternoon to see building extensions and slow progress of work. Sandwiches brought by whole school, as kitchen was not ready.

20th Nov. 1972
School granted holiday on the occasion of the Royal Silver Wedding Anniversary. School Dental Van moved on the school site by Mr Makins.

18th Dec. 1972
Kitchen staff moved equipment and supplies into kitchen extension. Physical education equipment moved to prepare for the painting/decorating.

19th Dec. 1972
School choir and band gave concert at Tuxford Methodist Chapel.

20th Dec. 1972
Christmas Service held in Tuxford Parish Church. Container meals system from Ollerton (during kitchen alterations) ceased. Painting and decoration of Physical Education Department commenced prior to Christmas Holidays.

8th Feb. 1973
Miss Green MBE, School Libraries, called to discuss fittings for new library. 20 pupils visited Balderton and Newark Hospitals with Mr Jeffcott and Mrs Pickering.

16th Feb. 1973
Books etc moved into new library block.

28th Mar. 1973
PC Ward visited 4th Year as part of Police/Scholar Relationship Scheme. Film shown. Mrs Pickering at Jessops Department Store, Nottingham for Careers Teacher Work Experience (5 days).

On Task, On Target *The story of the first fifty years of Tuxford School*

5th April 1973
School stage facilities as classroom affected by adult drama setting (rehearsal Thursday 5th April and performance 6th and 7th April). Classroom facilities restored Monday 10.30 a.m. April 9th. Mr Warren (Stephen George Architects) visited school extension to discuss move into New Block. New Art/Woodwork areas to free existing Art/Woodwork area for conversion.

9th April 1973
Final date for CSE folders to be submitted to examiner.

12th April 1973
School closed for Election purposes. Builders' conversion work area limited.

23rd May 1973
CSE Examinations - R/Studies I and II, Nursery Nursing and Child Care (Mode 3). 4th Year pupils' Parents Evening held at 7.30 p.m. in School Assembly Hall and Dining Area.

5th June 1973
Photographer from Retford Times newspaper called to photograph School Band.

7th June 1973
School closed and used for Rural District Election Polling.

14th June 1973
Hand over meeting of New Block, Library and School Kitchen. Mr Drew, Miss Green and Miss Whitlam and Mr Lee present. Many items still incomplete.
Miss M Granger visited Tuxford Primary School to see pupils due to transfer September 1973. Careers visit to CEGB Power Station at High Marnham by 12 girls and 18 boys.

9th July 1973
Stocktaking of books/equipment carried out a.m..

16th July 1973
Mr J Gold, Headmaster Newark C of E Secondary School, visited to see Cafeteria Choice of Meals system in operation.

17th July 1973
Mr Booth (Educational Adviser for Schools) called to discuss staffing, school roll for September and state of extensions/alterations building programme. Parents Evening held for New Intake, parents and pupils.

20th July 1973
Final Assembly Service held during afternoon
House Effort Trophy Winner: Newstead House; 2. Welbeck; 3. Thoresby; 4. Rufford Results of "Hush In" fund raising £465 (organised by Mr Martin and Mr Searle) banked in School Fund Deposit a/c to await next staff meeting in Autumn Term for allocation.

1976 Reorganisation:
Founding Principles Revisited

"This Authority has no doctrinaire approach to any of its problems… We are neither pro-comprehensive nor anti-comprehensive. We say, find the right solution for the right place.

"We have always believed that the most important thing is not the bricks and mortar, the desks and wallpaper, but the impact of the teachers on the children. The most important person in any school is the head teacher.

"We have said all along that the trouble with the comprehensive school is its great size, and that is the thing we have been frightened of. But we would have been fools indeed not to try to find the answer."

These words from Director of Education, J. Edward Mason, were reported in the Newark Advertiser of 8 July 1960 after the LEA announced that it was to build comprehensive schools at Ollerton and Kirkby-in-Ashfield – less than two years after Tuxford opened as a secondary modern. The Director's words would support a view that his time in charge of education for the county was a period of experiment to find a Nottinghamshire solution. However each experiment was replicated to such an extent that county solutions could now be viewed, ironically, as ideological; not partisan, but unwavering.

Establishing a chain of rural schools with attached farm units across the county was as remarkable an initiative as the pioneering of CLASP construction methods, but building one unit would have been an experiment; establishing a chain indicates a firm policy commitment. Unfortunately the policy, assessed in the light of subsequent events, was probably misguided because it was based on a false assumption of future economic development. Another county initiative was the establishment of a group of schools together on a single campus. The Newark Advertiser article refers to the example of Calverton where four schools shared a campus. This was another experiment that was replicated – in Worksop, for example. This model too was not entirely vindicated before being adopted. At Ollerton the over-sized impersonal, factory-like image of comprehensives was to be addressed by creating houses that would function to some extent as separate units within the wider school. However the Newark Advertiser article reports that new selective (grammar) schools were to be built in the county too and it was the opinion of Education Committee Chairman, Ald. A. Thompson, that schools sharing a campus was a model for future development that could prove to be superior "in many ways" to the comprehensive system. (1)

Six years later, the Newark Advertiser of 20 November 1966 carried a report on Tuxford School's Speech Day indicating that policies were changing. Headteacher Bernard Woodward's words are paraphrased: "The long-term plan was that the school would eventually be a rural comprehensive school and would deal with pupils from 11 to 16. The pupils could then transfer to sixth-year courses at Retford or Newark." (2) Such a matter-of-fact statement, but the implication should not be overlooked: less than a decade after the school had opened policy-makers were indicating that it was the wrong type of school.

The change of policy was instigated at national level. Circular 10/65 released in July 1965 was the initiative of recently appointed Education Secretary Anthony Crosland (and is sometimes called the Crosland Circular). It reflected the Labour government's commitment to replace selective schools, but stopped short of simply converting all schools into comprehensives. The delicate balance of power between government and LEAs made a "softly softly" approach expedient: the change was requested, not imposed. In practice, the Department of Education and Science used its financial muscle to make opposition to the change difficult: the DES refused to pay for any new secondary school which was not a comprehensive. It has to be said that Nottinghamshire, once again, was slow to react to a major national initiative. The building of Tuxford had come a decade after secondary schools were supposed to be established so it was to be expected that the change to comprehensive would happen twelve years after the circular from the ministry. In the meantime a Conservative government came to power (in June 1970) and education minister Margaret Thatcher allowed authorities to retain selective schools if so desired. However, this was quickly followed by the Local Government Act 1972 which set about reforming local government. New counties such as Humberside were created, and cities either merged with county councils as was the case with Nottingham or, like Greater Manchester, became metropolitan county councils. Elections were held to the new authorities in 1973, and the newly-elected groups then had a year as 'shadow authorities' to prepare for the handover on 1 April 1974.

One effect of unifying Nottinghamshire and Nottingham was to make the new authority more radical so "comprehensivisation" was pursued as a priority. A meeting for Tuxford School parents was arranged by the shadow LEA at the school on Wednesday January 16th 1974 - ten weeks before the official transfer of power. Incoming Education Committee Chairman, Mr B. Cairns, and Deputy Director of Education Mr Johnson outlined the timeline for Tuxford's change of status: "In September 1975 Newark becomes comprehensive and so the children to the south of the (catchment) area will take the eleven plus and go either to a lower tier comprehensive in Newark or to Tuxford Secondary School. In 1976 there will be no eleven plus and Tuxford Secondary School becomes a Comprehensive... The children already started on a course in Retford or Newark may, if they so wish, remain there to finish their course." (3)

The issue of starting a sixth form at Tuxford was discussed at the meeting – and a promise was made by the visitors: "In September 1976 there will be no purpose built sixth form accommodation at Tuxford School. The Council will give every encouragement to pupils wishing to remain at school and enter the sixth form and assures that special accommodation will be built as soon as numbers warrant it, before the main Comprehensive sixth form in 1981 if it is seen to be needed." The promise of a dedicated sixth form block was repeated a year later in the Retford Times when plans for Retford to go comprehensive were announced (4) – but the county council failed to honour its pledge. At least Tuxford was to have a sixth form - which was not foreseen back in 1966 when Mr Woodward addressed Speech Day.

In August 1975 the Retford Times revealed that Mr Woodward had been confirmed as headteacher of the comprehensive school. From January 1975 he had two terms leave from his normal duties to prepare for the change whilst his deputy, George Jeffcott, served as Acting Head. (5) There was much to prepare as the authority took the view that a completely new school was being opened. Each member of staff would have a job, but not necessarily his or her current job. A new staffing structure would be planned to take account of the new circumstances and staff would have to apply for posts within the structure. A new "Lower School Unit" would be opened to make the transition from primary to secondary education less traumatic for children. GCE O' level courses would be introduced and new staff would be recruited to lead some of these.

Management structures in the school were overdue for revison regardless of the change of status. The numbers on roll had increased so rapidly that, for example, the two deputy heads could no longer be personally responsible for all disciplinary issues. Whereas there had been 397 students in the school in 1972 before the school leaving age had been increased, in 1975 there were 585 and in 1976 there would be 685. Peggy Granger, who became a head of year in the new unit, recalled during a 2007 interview that: "The old system, which had been very rigid, began to crumble a little bit because we couldn't cope with the numbers." (6) A major element in the new staffing structure was to be the faculty: a group of subject departments linked together to organise courses and resources. A third deputy headteacher (Dennis Knox) was recruited to take responsibility for curriculum matters and it was he who would work with the heads of the four faculties to ensure that the more academic students due to arrive in September 1976 would be stretched and ultimately would achieve good results. The four faculties, as listed in the 1979 options booklet for fourth year students, were: Humanities and Languages; Science, Maths and Business Studies; Creative Design and Technology; Environmental, Community and Recreational Studies. (7)

Mick Keeling, appointed to teach Maths in the school in 1975 (and still doing so at the time of writing in 2007) recalled the appointment process for faculty heads: "When the school was reorganised as a comprehensive the faculty management model was introduced. Originally there were to be five faculties but I understand that County could not release enough funding to achieve this so four faculties were set up. Of course, this meant only four people in overall charge of all departments so there were bound to be a lot of disappointed if not disgruntled people at the end of the appointment process. To make matters worse the round of internal interviews, held first, resulted in no appointments being made so then the jobs were advertised nationally. External candidates came in such as Warren Cookson who ran the combined Maths and Science Faculty." (8)

Any major change is bound to be unsettling to many, but having a few colleagues with a grudge because they believed that they had been over-looked or treated shabbily must have been even more unsettling. Re-applying for jobs, preparation for new exams, higher expectations by parents and county, closer supervision by line managers, new staff in senior positions: all contributed to the tensions of reorganisation. Dennis Knox, former Curriculum Deputy Head, recalled how some of the long-established staff felt about the changes: "The secondary modern staff had previously had a great deal of freedom to teach what they wanted. They had a genuine desire to educate, but they didn't need to push either the children or themselves if they chose not to. Suddenly we brought in heads of faculty and new people from outside and it all changed fairly quickly. You can understand why there was some resistance to that. People soon came round and the new methods were adopted, but not all were happy about it. Of course the rest of the staff were keen. The Science and Maths staff led the way in introducing A' levels for example. Peter Rickerby who came in as Director of the Humanities and Languages Faculty was very keen. The emphasis from curriculum leaders was very much on 'What can we do for the children?' not on 'How can we change the staff?' " (9)

Headteacher Bernard Woodward must have appreciated how unsettling reorganisation would be when he opted to stay at the helm through the process. His colleague Elsie Pickering offered her view of his position: "Many people felt that he would retire rather than take on all the work of changing to a comprehensive, but he didn't. It was his school and he wanted to take the key decisions that would determine its future. He established subjects into broad faculties and he opened up a distinct Lower School unit so younger pupils could be largely segregated from older students." (10) However, Mick Keeling suggested that Mr Woodward had little room to manoeuvre because he was working to an LEA agenda: "…it was a County decision."

The next people to pass judgement on the changed status were the parents of primary school children eligible to transfer in September 1976. Retford still had grammar schools so able students from the north of Tuxford's catchment area could opt to try for places there. In the south the choice was between two comprehensives, Tuxford or one of the Newark lower tier schools feeding into former grammar schools. By autumn 1978, two years after reorganisation, new headteacher Keith Atkinson estimated that an approximate total of forty students were missing from the three full ability range year groups then in Tuxford School. He assumed that the parents of these children had more confidence in old grammar schools than in a reorganised secondary modern. (11) Therefore he was, understandably, very pleased to inform governors of the 1991 GCSE results: "These results amply illustrate the spectacular improvements made at the school since it became Comprehensive in 1976. It now comfortably outperforms the old Grammar Schools and is an excellent example of quality State Education." (12) Of course some parents had faith in the school from the start. Carol Brumpton recalls that she passed the eleven plus exam and was offered a place at a Retford grammar school, but she and her family chose Tuxford instead. (13)

Bernard Woodward's years as head were marked by several significant developments. It could be argued that the raising of the school leaving age had as profound an effect on school life as the change of status, for example. Mr Woodward had seen the school accommodation expand from one to three teaching blocks and the number of students on roll more than doubled. He was able to retire two years after reorganisation satisfied that the key features of the school were firmly established and that it had a bright future.

Sources

1   *Comprehensive… idea in Notts*, Newark Advertiser, 8 July 1960

2   *Tuxford School to be extended to rural all-in,* Newark Advertiser, 20 November 1966

3   *Reorganisation of Secondary Education: Tuxford Area*, Retford Times, 24 January 1974

4   *Plans for Comprehensive Education…*, Retford Times, 3 January 1975

5   *Preparing for Tuxford Comprehensive School,* Retford Times, 15 August 1975

6   *Looking Back*, Peggy Granger, Tuxford School Archive Papers, unpublished, 2007

7   *Which Course? Options Booklet 1979*, Tuxford School Publication, 1979

8   *Thirty Two Years & Three Headteachers*, Mick Keeling, Tuxford School Archive Papers, unpublished, 2007

9   *A View from Policy Committee*, Dennis Knox, Tuxford School Archive Papers, unpublished, 2007

10 *Mr Woodward's School*, Elsie Pickering, Tuxford School Archive Papers, unpublished, 2005

11 *Headteacher's Reports to Governing Body September 1978 and 1992,* Keith Atkinson, Tuxford School Archive Papers, unpublished

12 *Headteacher's Report to Governing Body September 1991*, Keith Atkinson, Tuxford School Archive Papers, unpublished

13 *Tuxford's first Comprehensive Intake*, Carol Brumpton, Tuxford School Archive Papers, unpublished, 2007

Tuxford 'Comprehensive 76'

Wide 'Catchment area preparing

IN September 1976, additional accommodation at the Tuxford County Secondary School will be ready for use and the school will become a comprehensive school for pupils aged 11-18.

Mr. B. W. Woodward ha been appointed Head Teache of the Comprehensive Scho and he and his staff are no preparing for the necessa changes. The school will p vide a wide variety of cour matching pupils' interests a aptitudes including cou leading to external exam tions.

From September 1976, Tuxford Comprehensive Sc will be the local secon school for children livin Bassetlaw and Newark Di

Reproduced courtesy of the *Retford Times*. 5 Dec 1975.

Mr Woodward's School, 1958 to 1978

BW Woodward

History, so far, hasn't been kind to Bernard Woodward, Tuxford School's first headteacher. Colleagues and students who only knew him during the latter days of his headship in the 1970s have gone on record to compare him unfavourably to his charismatic deputy, George Jeffcott, and when he retired, he had the misfortune to be succeeded as head by a man of extraordinary talent and energy - who went on to be awarded an M.B.E. for his services to education - so Mr Woodward's quieter, but real contribution to the school has gradually faded from the record. None of his correspondence, nor even a photograph, remained in school and little serious analysis of his achievements has been attempted – until now.

Bernard Woodward was headteacher of Tuxford County Secondary School from May 1958 (four months before it opened) until it disappeared at the end of August 1976; he was headteacher of Tuxford Comprehensive School from September 1976 until he retired in August 1978. From 1958 to 1972 he was also part-time Principal of Tuxford Educational Institute. During the Woodward years the number of students on roll more than doubled from 314 to 740 and staff numbers increased from 14 to 41. Some of the most significant events in the school's development also occurred during Mr Woodward's twenty years at the helm:

1958 - Tuxford School opened – a major investment in the town. Secondary education for all students in the area was assured. National press coverage and VIP visitors from home and abroad. Green school uniform introduced.

1965 - Certificate of Secondary Education introduced. A few students stayed in school for a fifth year to take the new exam. Decision taken to reorganise the school as a comprehensive.

1973 - Dramatic twenty percent increase in numbers: students could no longer leave during their fourth year; a fifth year in school was compulsory for all. The RoSLA Block (later

66

named the Trent Building) opened to provide new maths, art and craft rooms. A new library block (later the drama studio) also opened.

1976 - Tuxford School reorganised as a comprehensive: seventeen percent increase in numbers. Construction of Lower School building began – to house new Lower School Unit. Youth Centre also built. Several new staff were recruited and subject staff were grouped into faculties. Black blazers introduced. First school minibus bought.

1977 - The Lower School Block (later renamed the Clumber Building) completed. First and second year children were largely segregated from older students.

If we were to characterise the timeline as a journey, the initial period, 1958/59 to 1972/73 inclusive, was a stroll along a well-marked footpath whilst 1973/74 started a disorientating seven year climb up a winding hillside track. This two phase interpretation of the school's early history provides a useful insight into Mr Woodward's Tuxford career: for most of his time he was able to lead confidently through a familiar landscape, but during his final five years he found himself in unanticipated terrain so his leadership was not always so self-assured.

The path ahead of the first staff could not have been clearer: theirs was to be a specialist school for students aged 11 to 15, there was an emphasis on rural science within an attached farm unit, but a good level of education across a range of subjects was to be offered. No preparation for GCE O' level was permitted so students' work could have a practical or vocational bias. Bernard Woodward was well-prepared to assume the headship of such a school in 1958. His own school days had been spent as a boarder at Brewood Agricultural Grammar School in Staffordshire and he went on to be head of a rural science department. Tuxford was to be a secondary modern and he had twelve years experience teaching in secondary moderns. For four years he had been a deputy head and he felt himself ready for a headship. He knew Nottinghamshire because he had gained his degree in Nottingham. Tuxford was to be a community education provider offering evening classes throughout the district and Mr Woodward had the experience of organising further education courses at Chipping Norton. When he arrived he would not have needed county education officials to tell him about staffing, syllabuses, etc. He chose green and gold as the school colours because he believed them to be the colours of the countryside. He also chose an idyllic pastoral scene as the school's logo. He was enthusiastic and he had a clear vision of the climate he wished to create: "…within this School we are attempting to give all the children as much responsibility as they can take. We want boys and girls to achieve on the one hand a real independence and on the other standards of thought and conduct that are personal and sincere. If we are to educate men and women of responsibility, environment will be one of our chief instruments and I can feel already that within this School it is and will be an environment - a permeating environment of people - governors, parents, teachers and friends - Christian people with Christian standards…" (1)

Mr Woodward had personal insight into rural science and geography so he took great interest in these subject areas. He was responsible not only for staff appointments, but also for the timetable. He had a clear vision of the type of staff he wanted: "…the teacher with humanity within his interest is likely to be far more influential with children than the technically efficient instructor." A sense of humour, a willingness to contribute to staffroom life and an empathy for others were sought from candidates. However, he was very formal in many ways and was never addressed in public by his staff by any other name than Sir. Similarly he never called colleagues by their first names. Perhaps he was reflecting the more formal society of the 1950's or perhaps he was influenced by his own boarding school upbringing. Nevertheless,

67

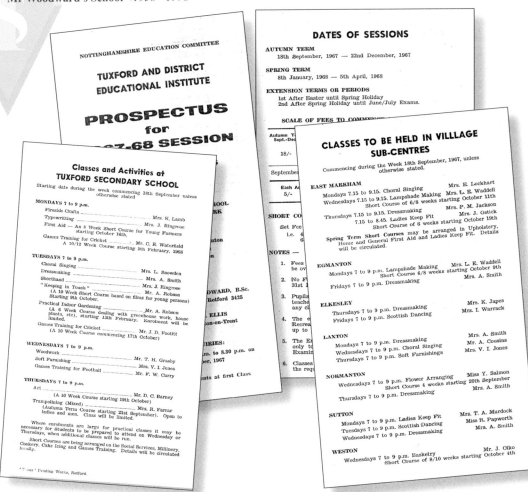

early colleagues reported that he was astute in understanding people and their concerns. He is certainly on record as saying "Relationships between people are of the utmost importance." Mr Woodward was a sincere Christian and one way in which he promoted Christianity in school was to name the four school houses after patron saints of local churches: St Lawrence (Norwell) St Nicholas (Tuxford) St Oswald (Dunham-on-Trent) and St. Peter (Gamston). His school assemblies were always acts of worship – but very formal in tone.

One of the responsibilities placed on students was to keep the farm unit working during school holidays. Several answered the call for volunteers. A different kind of trust was demonstrated by the absence of locks on cupboards and lockers. Senior students were appointed as prefects and entrusted with maintaining good order during breaks. Students could also be given occasional jobs - such as cleaning a teacher's car, preparing refreshments for visitors or washing the staff tea cups - requiring a level of commitment, responsibility and commonsense. Although students were free from exam pressure and untroubled by much homework, educational success was important in the early school. Several students went on to take A' levels in FE colleges after they left the school and they had successful careers in the professions. Mr Woodward told early parents, "An essential part of education is giving encouragement, and courage to believe that successful standards are possible."

The school's punishment book shows that Mr Woodward wielded the cane when necessary to maintain standards. He delegated much of the responsibility for discipline to George Jeffcott, his deputy, and to Meg Graham, the Senior Mistress, but he still dealt with incidents himself. In the early days he was much more active in the daily life of the school than he became in later years. He helped and advised staff, visited subject areas and ordered equipment when needed. He also helped individual students as Peggy Granger recalled: "Mr Woodward… took a particular interest in the welfare of the less able or less prominent children. I had a first year child who appeared to be learning very little and Mr Woodward came into the classroom one morning, saw this child's handwriting and said, "I don't know how Miss Granger reads that. Come to me at lunch time." So the lad did - and he taught him to write properly." (2)

Lunchtimes provided an important opportunity for social or extra-curricular education. Denise Brackenbury recalled them with enthusiasm almost fifty years after she experienced them: "For lunch I would sit at a table already laid out with tablecloth and cutlery with six other girls and Mr Jeffcott. We looked forward to our school dinners and for about a shilling a day we could buy a meal which would consist of meat and two vegetables and a custardy pudding. After a good dinner I was part of a privileged group of girls to take dancing lessons – jive lessons in fact, with Mr Jeffcott. I looked forward to these sessions as we could listen to records as well – Billy Fury was my hero! We had dances in those days too. Mr Jeffcott organised these and we could show off our jive technique." (3) As for the head teacher, Peggy Granger explained how he spent his lunchtime: "Mr Woodward played squash or something - with Jeff or whoever. He was very much a sportsman, but he tried to take some exercise at lunch time."

Mr Woodward's dedication to his job was remembered by Brenda Maw, a teaching colleague from 1958: "(The Head) would go anywhere to look at the children's work. Once there was an open day at Worksop one Saturday afternoon and our children had work there and he wanted the staff to visit to support them. However, Mr Jeffcott said he wouldn't go." (4) The head was certainly committed to working evenings sometimes too. At the end of the school day most people, both staff and students, could go home with plenty of time for family life and leisure but the building had an evening role as an Educational Institute for the community. Mr Woodward, as its Principal, did much of the organising himself. The 1967 prospectus reveals that village sub-centres provided courses at East Markham, Egmanton, Elkesley, Laxton, Normanton, Sutton and Weston. The courses offered at the school or the sub-centres were popular and they included Dress Making, Scottish Dancing, Ladies Keep Fit and Basketry. Mr Woodward enrolled everyone personally and the prospectus included his home telephone number so anyone interested in enrolling could contact him. In the evenings, as his daughter Veronica explained, he would use his car to ferry course leaders to the sub-centres if required.

All the evidence suggests that Mr Woodward was very much the driving force in the school at the start. He enjoyed showing off the building and the farm unit to many visitors from home and abroad. The school was fulfilling its planned role and parents generally were very supportive - although the first school uniform only lasted for eight years according to Peggy Granger: "When I started teaching at Tuxford in 1966 the uniform was beginning to slip because there wasn't much help for parents to get uniform at the time. Some of the children were farm labourers' children and farm labourers were having a pretty tough time then, so you couldn't really enforce it. You tried but you couldn't." Another concession by Mr Woodward was the renaming of school houses in December 1971: "It was the tempo of the times. We stopped calling the subject Religious Knowledge and started calling it Religious Education, it wasn't scripture or denominational anymore. A suggestion was made that we should rename the school houses to drop the names of local churches." (2) It is difficult today to view the change as an improvement. At least the churches were local to the school catchment area, whereas their replacements, estates in the Dukeries, had little connection to the lives of Tuxford students.

The second, more difficult, stage in the school's journey – and Mr Woodward's – was the consequence of changes imposed from outside. We have seen in an earlier section that the introduction of CSE in 1965 led to some disquiet in the staffroom, but the effect of raising the school leaving age was to be more profound. Previously the numbers on roll had remained fairly steady, around 400, from 1960 to 1972 then in 1973 there were suddenly one hundred additional pupils in school – older ones, and many of them resented being there for another year. Two years later there were 585 students and in 1976 another 100 as the school became a comprehensive.

Peggy Granger remembered the problems that arose from rapid expansion: "The old system, which had been very rigid, began to crumble a little bit because we couldn't cope with the numbers... We actually taught classes on the landings in the Tower Block on occasions. That was a nightmare." New systems had to be developed to adjust to the rapid increase in numbers. Mr Woodward at the age of 58 had to lead the school in new directions. Suddenly public examinations took on a new importance and an effort was made to reintroduce school uniform. New syllabuses had to be developed and Mr Woodward had to work with architects and builders as first the RoSLA block then Lower School were constructed. The specialist rural science status of the school was quietly played down and craft teaching facilities were upgraded significantly by building the RoSLA block.

Introduction of the new uniform in 1976 did not go smoothly. Carol Brumpton was one of the pupils who had to wear it: "We were the first intake to move into the new 'Lower School' (Clumber Building). We were also the first to wear the new uniform: black blazers, grey skirts (as long as we could get and very tight) or trousers with, at first, gold Trutex shirts for both sexes that were soon changed to white. The years above us did not have a uniform. They were smartly dressed in clothes of their own choice. We were even more conspicuous than previous first years and were picked on out of lessons so much that we stayed on the tennis courts. Let's just say that older kids soon found that blackboard chalk contrasted very well with our black blazers. Sometimes there was more chalk on us than on the boards." (5) The uniform was not enforced across the whole school so it didn't last long. Peggy Granger suggested why: "The uniform was re-introduced when we went comprehensive. It was a black blazer: I think that was the children's choice, they preferred black. But it didn't stay long because blazers had gone out of fashion in most schools. Students were mostly wearing anoraks because of going across the site in bad weather."

Despite the changes the essential culture lived on. Liz Bradshaw started at the school in 1974 and she remembered a colleague's assessment of the place: "Craft teacher Tom Grasby came to meet me and knew my family. He said: 'If you get a job here I think you will be all right – and you will find that it's like Butlins here.' " (6) When she started she got to know the head quite well: "I was fortunate because I got on well with Mr Woodward. Often he would come into my room and was keen to find out how everything was working in my area. He was always a serious person and he would offer advice in a fatherly manner. He would say: 'If I

70

were you I would try it like this…' When I requested a new bookcase he came to measure the space where I wanted it and then concluded: 'Yes, I think that will be all right.' Then he would look through various catalogues."

During this period of rapid change deputy head George Jeffcott found himself increasingly responsible for much of the day to day running of the school whilst Mr Woodward worked with county advisers and with senior staff on key development decisions. For two terms in 1976 "Jeff" was Acting Headteacher. Several new staff recruited at the time had much more daily contact with Mr Jeffcott than with Mr Woodward and it was to him they turned to sort out any problems. Dennis Knox, also deputy head from 1976 saw the extent of Mr Jeffcott's intervention: "Jeffcott never undermined him or criticised him – he was very careful about this – but Jeffcott was very much in charge at that time when I came. Sometimes kids would come to Mr Woodward and he should have punished them, but he would say, 'All right I will let you off this time.' Jeffcott would wait round the corner and grab the kids. He told them, 'The headmaster has let you off, but I am not going to' and he would give them the stick if necessary. He ran the school in that way. He was a good disciplinarian. This intervention did not bother Mr Woodward in the slightest. He was a very easygoing chap and good to work with because he let you do what you felt needed to be done." (7) Dennis Knox's theory is that the head was happy to delegate at this stage in his career: "He was near retirement – and I suppose near retirement we all relax a little and take it a bit easier for the last year or so. We had great respect for him and I got on with him very well."

One of the features of Tuxford School culture – a key democratising influence but not always attractive as a quality – is iconoclasm. No-one is allowed to become too grand or too precious because they will be ridiculed. This trait can be traced back to Mr Woodward's early years as head and he was certainly an early target for it. Brenda Maw recalled: "Bernie had several endearing idiosyncrasies such as adding 'in fact' to sentences unnecessarily. He would say, 'It's a nice day, in fact.' Johnny Bee (another early teacher) used to sit near to me in the staffroom and keep count of how many 'in facts' were used." (4) Later staff counted how many times he included 'er' in sentences and they gave him the nickname 'Bunny', presumably a corruption of Bernie. These examples might suggest that Mr Woodward was not respected. As we have noted already, this is not true. Everyone I have questioned who knew him has agreed that he was a perfect gentleman, quite formal and a little serious, but very considerate of staff. Peggy Granger has said of his years in charge, "I always felt Mr Woodward was fully in control - but quietly." (2) A later colleague, Cathie Town, suggested that the head almost encouraged staff to vent their frustrations: "He never went into the staff room unless he was invited as he felt that the staff needed somewhere to moan without being worried that the Head would hear it!" (8)

The teasing of colleagues was a feature of Tuxford staffroom humour from the start and Cathie Town offered several examples of fun at Mr Jeffcott's expense: "…'Jeff' Jeffcott, was always trying to set standards for staff. When Mick Keeling came for interview, for example, Jeff afterwards said, 'He can get his bloomin' hair cut' - but history proved that Mick never did!

"Jeff would often have me in for a 'pep talk' and tell me if I was doing anything he thought inappropriate, or I was getting too full of myself. Back in those times there was no uniform, and mini-skirts were the fashion. I wore them myself, and I was often told by Mr Jeffcott that my skirts were too short. Previously neither female staff nor female students were allowed to wear trousers; Jo Grocock fought and won that right for us.

"Some would moan about Jeff, but overall he was very respected and I thought he was

Back row: Unknown, John Freeborough, John Forster, Ron Hardwick, Tom Grasby, Jerry Ball, Gordon Ellis.
Middle Row: Unknown, Unknown, Audrey Anderson, Phil Chambers, Pat Foulds.
Front Row: Mavis Paling, Lena Snowden, George Jeffcott, Bernard Woodward, Meg Graham, Unknown, Mary Wooten (School secretary). Photograph taken in 1964.

wonderful. He had no shades of grey, everything was 'black or white'. He always treated everyone the same, and everyone knew where the 'Line' was! He taught maths and no student ever wanted to change groups. On one occasion he left a complete year group in the hall to sit in absolute silence. He went off to the staff room to have a cigarette before coming back – and when he returned they were still sitting there in total silence. That is what you call well respected. However, for me his most endearing features were his beautiful blue eyes!

"One day in assembly the usual teachers sat on the stage, and the sun was shining in such a way that it spotlighted Mr Jeffcott's chair. Pete Searle, never one to miss an opportunity, commented to him, 'I know you think the sun shines out of your backside, but I didn't think I'd ever see it!' Jeff could always take a joke, and was well supported by everyone.

"Thursday night was his rugby night at Newark Rugby Club, so by Friday lunchtime he would usually fall asleep. Not to miss an opportunity we would tie his shoe laces together around the chair legs, and Pete Searle once made him a sign saying "SLEEPING – DO NOT DISTURB" and stuck it to him."

Cathie Town, like Liz Bradshaw, started teaching at the school in 1974. Liz – then Miss Fox - recalled that her teaching career got off to a shaky start: "My first day was a nerve-racking experience.

"My very first lesson was taken in the rural studies area – complete with smelly wellies and gerbils. The small animals had been with pupils during the Summer holiday, but now reunited they were very excited and making a disturbance in my lesson with new intake pupils. One girl put her hand up and told me: 'Miss, one has got on top of the other and is killing it.' However, a boy soon told her what was really happening without sparing her blushes or mine!

"For my second lesson I moved to what in the end was the school office (overlooking the amphitheatre). At one end it had a small kitchen with two cookers and two sinks. My group consisted of about eight 15-year-olds and I wanted to do some practical work with them although it was obvious that the room had not been put to such use for ages. We started by cleaning the area, but when a tap was turned on it would not turn off again. Soon a human chain had to be formed with buckets, bowls and anything else that would hold water to prevent the sink overflowing before the caretaker arrived. Edward Cookson had actually worked for my father so when he surveyed the scene he simply said: 'Elizabeth, what the bloody hell do you think you are doing?' He was followed closely by Deputy Head George Jeffcott, who said much the same. How I kept the job I don't know – and I had to go home at lunch to change.

"After school had finished I set off down the school corridor full of high spirits – happily whistling to myself. However the Senior Mistress Mrs Graham caught me and gave me a good telling off. 'Excuse me, Miss Fox, I feel that I ought to point out that we disapprove of staff whistling in school. We certainly do not feel that it is ladylike conduct.'

"Mr Woodward, according to his wife Una, collectively nicknamed Liz and Cathie "The Girls". He followed their progress – and that of all of his staff with interest. Some staff were unhappy when they failed to be appointed to specific roles in the reorganised school, but they did not blame Mr Woodward for this. In fact they were impressed that he had chosen to steer the school through the process of transformation when he could have opted for retirement. In doing so he ensured that his influence remained in school for years after he left in 1978. True, it was no longer the school that he had chosen to lead and there is little doubt that his participation in the life of the place had diminished in latter years, but he was in a position to appoint staff to the comprehensive and he would ensure that they shared essential characteristics with established colleagues. The key features of Mr Woodward's staff - informality, enterprise, light-hearted scepticism, a sense of humour and a concern for others - became embedded in the school's organisational culture. These are still Tuxford qualities at the time of writing, in 2007.

Tuxford School maintained its sense of fun and good humour throughout the period of change – even through the upheaval of reorganisation. Paradoxically it was the very serious Bernard Woodward who deserves at least some of the credit for this. He never lost the belief that the school would be a success if relationships were right and he was convinced that the learning environment was as important as the syllabus to students' progress. Perhaps Mr Grasby was right, perhaps Mr Woodward's school was like Butlins: a well-organised place (on the surface at least) devoted to providing a full programme of activities.

Sources

1   *A Talk to Parents, Bernard Woodward*, Tuxford School Archive Papers, unpublished, 2007

2   *Looking Back*, Peggy Granger, Tuxford School Archive Papers, unpublished, 2007

3   *Schooldays 1958-59*, Denise Brackenbury, Tuxford School Archive Papers, unpublished, 2005

4   *Three Early Teachers Remember*, Brenda Maw, Colin Maw, Gordon Ellis, Tuxford School Archive Papers, unpublished, 2006

5   *Tuxford's first Comprehensive Intake*, Carol Brumpton, Tuxford School Archive Papers, unpublished, 2007

6   *An interview with Liz Bradshaw* (née Fox) 2005, Tuxford School Archive Papers, unpublished, 2005

7   *A View from Policy Committee*, Dennis Knox, Tuxford School Archive Papers, unpublished, 2007

8   *Sunlight and mini-skirts,* Cathie Town, Tuxford School Archive Papers, unpublished, 2005

One of my other interests in school was taking part in the school choir. I loved music and had a real passion for singing and Mrs Snowden entered us for a singing competition almost every week. There were always groans from the other schools when they saw the Tuxford team arrive because of our winning performances on a regular basis.

Extract from *Schooldays 1958-59* by Denise Brackenbury.

Music with Mrs Snowden

Mrs. Snowden was a lovely lady with a wonderful voice. Being in the school choir we would, as a treat, sing modern songs: one of our favourites was "To know, know, know him, is to love, love, love him", which we would rehearse over and over again. I remember how Mrs. Snowden would warn the choir members not to laugh when we were in assemblies - but the stage stairs would let us down by creaking, and someone would always receive that look, the "dead eye", from her. I always prayed it would never be me.

Extract from *Memories of Tuxford School 1958-60* by Shirley Knowles.

Retirement Reminiscences (1958 – 1978)

Written by Bernard Woodward at the end of his term as headteacher

A *is for* **Admissions**
Admissions of pupils have now reached the total of 2,944. 313 pupils were admitted on the first day when the school opened.

John Pepper - 1958-1959, attended three evening classes as well as day school, later qualified in engineering for the National Coal Board – returned annually to school over many years to spend a full day with us. Married with two children living in Ollerton and occupied in voluntary work.

Elizabeth Gould - (best friend Gillian Baumber from Normanton) emigrated to Australia before 18th birthday. Career in Banking in Perth, Western Australia. June 1978 Elizabeth returned to Low Marnham for wedding – husband Mr Irwin Salve (Australian). Before returning to Melbourne she telephoned her good wishes to the School and members of staff whom she knew between 1963 and 1968.

B *is for* **Burglars and Break ins**
Two young burglars from the North were caught at Lincoln with a portable B & W television set from the school. One burglar gave himself up at Leicester after he had spent the small amount of money stolen (from Tuxford and two other schools) and decided to rest in police custody in order to get his next meal!

Beards - Three members of staff returned to school after the summer holiday 1974 with growths of beards! Changing fashion, a shortage of blades, a bet - or a coincidence!

C *is for* **Cyclists/Motor Cyclists**
In 1958 42 pupils cycled from East Markham. 2 members of staff C & B Maw travelled in motorcycle and sidecar. Cycling revival in 1974 - tour of all contributory villages by teaching staff sponsored to raise funds for school minibus. Mr Searle, Mr Martin, Mr Longden, Mr Parkinson, Mr Richardson, Mrs Paling and Mrs Grindle on cycles, Mr Ives on moped.

Camping - The first school pupils involved in camping went to Yorkshire in 1961. Other boys' camping expeditions to Ashover, Derbyshire with Mr Jeffcott and Mr Grasby. Girls camping to Collingham with Mrs Graham as part of the Duke of Edinburgh Award Scheme.

D *is for* **Doctor Tattersall**
Doctor Tattersall has been involved in school medical examination, innocs/ vaccination for nearly twenty years.

Discus - thrown 125ft 1in by Robert Brackenbury (64-68) at the *All England Sports* at Peterborough.

E *is for* **Employment Officers**
Now Careers Officers – many have had long association with the school. Outstanding personal service was given to all families in the school area by Jack Whitworth – now involved in the Work Orientation Unit at North Notts College of Further Education.

Examinations- The school was first involved in preparing pupils for the *Nottinghamshire Leaving Certificate* examinations. Mrs Rawson who has recently returned as a supply teacher was involved in preparing Home Economics pupils from 1959-63 for their exams in that subject.

F *is for* **Foot and Mouth Disease**
Foot and Mouth Disease in the Tuxford District in 1960/61 resulted in the exclusion of pupils from the Farm Unit to prevent the spread of the disease amongst livestock in the farms of our area.

Fire Engines - Fire engines were called to an emergency in a smoke filled Home Economics room one dinnertime – an overheated drying cabinet (and tea towels) resulted in the electric power supply being cut off.

G *is for* **Grandmas and Granddads**
Grandmas and granddads on the teaching staff – time moves on – Mrs Snowden has six grandchildren. Mrs Chambers has three, Mr Jeffcott has two, Mr Woodward has one. Bottom of the League!

H *is for* **Hairdresser's Son**
Hairdresser's son – Stephen Hague (1958-62) came to Tuxford for his Rural Studies and farming interests – then joined his father's trade! Studied Art/ Craft in his off time from work and attended Doncaster College. Purchased a horse and caravan, travelled the highways and byways of Norfolk county – returned to the Mansfield area and took a full time course of Art/Craft at Mansfield College of Art. Now Stephen has a Pottery Studio at Thoresby Hall – lives at Bothamsall and has a great interest in vintage cars!

I *is for* **Influenza**
Influenza virus "got at" Mr Jeffcott in October 1958 – first absent staff member! Later in same school year half the school absent with flu. The Library became a sick bay for pupils who were ill after arrival at school. A second year form were the centre of infection nearly 100% absent – but the other forms and staff affected in varying degrees.

J *is for* **Jersey Calves**
Jersey calves Lady and May were bought in 1958. Raised to start the Jersey herd of Tuxford Lady and Tuxford May. May was sold at Newark market. Descendants of Lady are still with us: Tuxford Lady Sue and now her recent calf still to be named.

One chief - of a party of Sudanese Chieftains to visit the school was not at all interested in cattle at Tuxford. He said he has 20,000 cattle of his own in the Sudan. The British Council Official who accompanied the visitors told us that this chief had murdered his uncle to obtain his cattle. He was very interested in lady members of staff being in a staff room!

K *is for* **Kite Flying**
Kiteflying Japanese professors, lecturers and teachers insisted on demonstrating their skills on the school field and invited pupils to try also.

L *is for* **Lamp**
The Miners' Lamp in the glass case was donated to the school by Mr Fox of the National Coal Board in 1966.

M *is for* **Mobile Dental Clinic**
Mr Makins and Mrs Palethorpe have visited the school since 1968. Prior to this pupils were issued with special bus passes to go into Retford or Newark – the bus journey in, treatment and return took a whole school day in each case!

Music Festivals - Many Music Festivals have been held over the years at Brigg, Lincoln and Worksop, in which the school choir, soloists and bands have been involved in winning cups, shields and certificates with Music Maestro (or Mistress) Mrs Snowden.

One pupil - David Cregg 1958–61, so concerned at his forgetfulness on the way to Brigg Festival borrowed a green and gold tie from a girl pupil in order to appear 'correctly' dressed and in full school uniform for the Festival. David later trained as a Catering Officer journeying to and from South Africa on the Union/Castle line – sent picture postcards from Durban. Latest news, he's now in charge of a hotel in the Birmingham area.

N *is for* **Nursing**

The Nursing Careers Training Officer from Worksop – astonished the careers staff and pupils when he gave first talk – all were expecting a lady – instead a Mr Fenn Nursing Tutor arrived in his white coat. The first pupil to complete a full SRN course and gain that qualification was Enid Billington from Sibthorpe Hill. After experience in Nottingham General Hospital she went to work as a trained nurse for an industrial firm working in Algeria, N Africa.

O *is for* **Ornithology Club 1965-1971**

The Ornithology Club involved both parents and pupils coming to joint evening meetings (parents provided transport for their sons and daughters). Mr Robson and his club members worked with the County taxidermist to supplement the museum specimens now on loan to schools.

P *is for* **Primary Schools**

Sutton On Trent and Tuxford who are this year celebrating their hundred years of existence were built of brick cast. "CLASP" prefabricated structures of which our main school building is an example were designed with a short span of life in mind. 20 years perhaps! The first architect, Alan Goodman gave this figure as his estimate! 1958… 1978 …??

Q *is for* **Quercus Robus**

Quercus robus is the oak tree in the Amphitheatre around which the main school was designed and built (1956/8). The leaves from this tree were used by one Home Economics teacher and pupils for wine making.

R *is for* **Rugby Training Sessions**

Rugby training sessions were held in the middle of August holiday. Mr Jeffcott and Mr Perry met pupils who cycled back to school. Ross, Keith (1963–67) was renowned for his skiffle groups which held evening practices in school.

S *is for* **Sark**

Sark – one of the channel islands to which Piers Beaumont 1966/68 and his father Signeur Beaumont returned when the Dame of Sark (grandma) died. The Queen recently visited Sark and no doubt Piers was in the reception party. Piers and his family lived at Askham.

T *is for* **Teachers**

Bless'em all – the long, the short and the tall!

Technology - The changes since 1958 have been staggering. In 1958 the school had one sound projector, one filmstrip projector and one tape recorder. No television set. Half the cost of the first Black and White set had to be raised by the school in 1964. Radio programmes were received by a Trix Master set in the Headteachers room. Loudspeakers were plugged into classroom sockets.

U *is for* **"Urdu"**
"Urdu" a form of Hindustani language spoken in India - and heard in Tuxford School corridors and staffroom daily when Mrs Snowden met colleague Mr John Forster – teacher from 1958-66.

V *is for* **Vine**
Vine in the school greenhouse – started in 1959 by a grapevine 'eye' brought by Sheila Middleton, pupil from Dunham.

Visits - Visits can be unusual.
A series of study visits entitled "Man and the Community". were organised for school pupils in the town of Newark. Group leaders were trainee clergymen from that House of Sacred Mission, Kelham. All groups were adequately supervised in their day's programme – except the group of pupils allocated to go to Hole's Brewery!

W *is for* **Weather**
And its effects on staff and pupils. Mr Jeffcott stranded in snow in Sheffield, 1962. 51 Pupils stranded in school until 7:00 pm in 1969. Gales blew down the end brick wall of the games barn, in 1962 (5 other school barns also damaged). Fog in 1963 resulted in a 2 hours door-to-door dropping off of pupils around the villages after a visit to the Vienna Boys Choir visit in Nottingham 1973.

Weighing Machine - The weighing machine in the Farm Unit broke a teachers' nose in 1958. The handle was not locked over!

X *is for* **Xmas Poultry**
Plucking and dressing in the week before Xmas as the school did not have a deep freeze until 1969. Mr Jeffcott was always the "General" in charge of this annual event.

Y *is for* **Young Farmers Rallies and Activities**
Frederick Forshaw 1958–62 from Sutton on Trent, arranged for an ITV camera crew to film pupils working in the farm unit in August 1962. Frederick is now a Computer Programmer at County Hall, Nottingham.

Z *is for* **Zoo Man**
Zoo man (George Consdale) talked to young pupils and let them handle snakes, etc in the main school hall. He also opened the new Primary School at Dunham on Trent.

80

1968 Anniversary of Tuxford's Royal Charter

Mrs E Pickering

Mrs M Graham fo

Mrs P Chambers

Mr A Harrison fo

Mr J Herrett for

Mr J Nicholson f

Rev T W Swift fo

Like Ghosts at Cockcrow
Written and directed by Peggy Granger.

1. **Early Middle Ages**
   Alison
   Ben   Christine Pocklington
   Tom   Andrew Cook
   Jake   Peter Martin
   Hugh   Alex Herbert
      David Westhorpe

2. **The Later Middle Ages**
   Old Katherine
   Ann   Carol Sampson
   Martin   Margaret Parker
      John Marshall

3. **The Tudors**
   Guy, a minstrel   Peter Lilliman
   Rob, a minstrel   Stephen Matthews
   Mistress Padgett   Judith Spencer
   Susan Childe   Angela Barsby
   Mistress Taylor   Linda Hammond
   Children   Patricia Meppem, Susan Thompson
      Angela Dronfield, Susan Davies
      Jane Thornhill Susan Buckingham
   Bishop   Angela Gavin, Karen Barr
   Princess   Nigel Gash
      Susan Batterby

4. **The Plague**
   Stranger

7. **The Fire 1701**
   Jeremy Watmough
   (Sexton of Tuxford)

8. **Helen Walker 1737**
   A Scottish Girl
   Mr Brewitt
   Mr Marklow
   A traveller

9. **The Rebel Stone 1746**
   William
   Samuel
   Robert

10. **The Nineteenth Century**
   Samuel
   James
   Tom   Mark
   Mary   Pete
   Anne   Peter

Some Historical and Imaginary Scenes from Tuxford's Past. Friday 10th May 1968.

Staff and Students of 1978

harles Keith Atkinson became the second headteacher of Tuxford School at the beginning of September 1978. Appropriately, the big film of September 1978 was 'Grease'; in the minds of his many former students he will be forever associated with two wider interests, promoting excellence in sport and the enjoyment of popular music. It soon became apparent that his style of leadership would be very different from his predecessor's; his presence would be felt daily throughout the school at every level of its operation.

Teacher Mick Keeling recalled the day of Mr Atkinson's appointment: "I was on bus duty and was slightly surprised to see Acko down there too. He was on bus duty and he had only come for his interview! Afterwards I realised this showed his attention to detail, his concern for the small routines of school as well as the core ones and his interest in seeing the children in their environment. I remember saying to him, 'If you want it mate, good luck!' and of course he did get it. And his appointment was the best thing that ever happened to this school and not even moving to a new building can have as big an impact." (1)

News of Mr Atkinson's appointment and a brief outline of his career appeared in the Retford Times of May 5th. He gained a little teaching experience in 1956 and 1957, at South County Junior School in West Bridgford which he had attended as a pupil, before studying for a B.A. and Diploma in Education at Durham University. From 1961 to 1964 he taught at Toothill Secondary Modern, Bingham. He was Head of Geography (and subsequently Head of Humanities) at Wilsthorpe Comprehensive in Derbyshire from 1964 to 1974 then served as Deputy Head of South Wolds Comprehensive from May 1974 until the end of August 1978. (2)

1978 was the year when the first 'test tube' baby, Louise Brown, was born. Exiled Bulgarian journalist Georgi Markov was killed in London in September by Eastern bloc assassins who used an umbrella to inject poison into his leg. 1978 was also the year when there were three Popes: Paul VI died in August, his successor, John Paul, died at the end of September so a little known Polish cardinal surprisingly became the very successful John Paul II.

The country had changed considerably during the twenty years since the school had opened. Between 1960 and 1970 the number of people employed in agriculture had fallen by 25 percent (although production had increased by 40 percent over the same period). Locally, work at High Marnham power station and at various local coal mines had attracted new people into the area, particularly to housing estates in Elkesley and Tuxford. Trade unions were powerful in 1978 (the year before Mrs Thatcher came to power as Britain's first woman prime minister) and disputes in the workplace were not uncommon. Disputes in the home were quite common too judging by divorce statistics: in 1961 there had been 27,224 divorces in Great Britain; by 1972 this had risen to 124,556 – the year after the 1969 Divorce Reform Act came into effect. Another social change, discussed in an earlier section, was the raising

Richard Martin, rural studies teacher.

of the school leaving age with effect from 1973 so young people in their mid-teens could put off career decisions for longer and, consequently, had more spare time than earlier students of the same age. Entry into the adult world of work was postponed for the high proportion who would have previously opted out of continued studies.

The various social changes created incidents and tensions within the community around Tuxford School. Former student Carol Brumpton recalled rivalry between young people in the rapidly expanding local communities: "I mixed with the Elkesley crowd quite a bit, so I'd regularly get on the bus with them and found some of them were a rough lot. There were issues between Tuxford and Elkesley youths as well as between Ollerton and Tuxford ones… The Ollerton rivalry often encroached into the youth club and older boys would come over to disrupt the youth club at Tuxford." (3) She also remembered that organisers of dances at Sutton on Trent had to cope with rowdy young people from across the area.

In school there was very little trouble from students, but before the reintroduction of school uniform some chose clothing to declare their status and to reflect their attitudes. Carol Brumpton recalled: "Some of the bad older guys wore smart jackets and brogue shoes and things like that. These guys looked distinctively older and quite sinister because of their code of dress. I think school uniform does make a difference to prevent this kind of gang identity being expressed."

Of course the vast majority of young people then, as now, were sensible and co-operative. Maths teachers Dennis Knox and Mick Keeling who started working at the school in the mid 70s formed favourable impressions of the students of the time. Mr Knox remembered: "My early impressions were how good the children were…" (4) Mr Keeling agreed: "There were very few discipline problems in school in those days. Any that we did have Jeff would sort. I think the rogues then you might describe now as a bit naughty compared to some of the twisted characters that can be found in schools these days due to changes in society." (1)

However Carol Brumpton remembered older students from the perspective of a younger child: "When we started some fourth and fifth year guys were really tough, but by the third year, after Mr Atkinson arrived, I would say that things were settling down quite well and noticeably it was better." (3) The arrival of Keith Atkinson clearly made an impression on her: "When Mr Atkinson, ('Count' or 'Drac' as in Count Dracula) arrived, I was scared to death of him. Even though Mr Jeffcott was scary he was much more so."

Another insight into student life provided by Carol was the use of dinner tokens as a type of currency: "There was a dinner token black market in school. In fact it was rife everywhere and on a Monday morning there'd be fourth and fifth years exchanging their dinner tokens for money, cigarettes, sweets - anything like that. If someone was desperate for a dinner token they would be overcharged by 20 to 30p to get their money back and some of the traders weren't rogues at the school either. They had simply got their own enterprise going."

Early PE lessons were also recalled by Carol Brumpton – and her anecdote shows a more sensitive side to the students of the 1970s: "I was traumatised at the end of our first Games lesson. It was quite a funny age when we girls were developing and Mrs Frearson shouted, 'Right girls, shower everyone.' She was trotting about while we were all going 'Mmm, we don't want to do this. Perhaps we could just drop our towel and run through…' Then to our horror she stripped off and showered with the girls as though it was absolutely the norm! - and we were all wide-eyed and embarrassed. A few girls just got on with it, but there were certainly a lot of us who'd not seen our mums like it. There were excuse letters three foot high every week after that: it was off-putting just to do PE because you needed to have a shower."

Carol cited an eventful trip to Dovedale during her second year in school as an insight into student attitudes and behaviour at the time that Mr Atkinson arrived at Tuxford. There was excitement because they were going on a coach trip – but the departure was delayed because a few students arrived late. The coach developed mechanical problems on the outward journey, but eventually got them to their destination. The teachers would already have been frustrated by the journey time - then over the lunch break the students decided to play a practical joke on them: they excused themselves in ones and twos for various plausible reasons then hid until only about a third of the party was left. Carol reported that: "Mr Foreman got extremely cross and stamped his feet."

Even though the school had been a comprehensive for two years when Mr Atkinson arrived it still did not attract all of the gifted students from within the catchment area. Teacher Julie Hethershaw recalled: "…until about 1980 the school lost a lot of talented students to the former grammar schools in Retford and Newark because we were still regarded as a rural secondary modern built around a farm unit." (5)

Carol Brumpton's observations of staff are as perceptive as her insights into student attitudes. She provided the following descriptions of some of the people who taught her:

"Mr Rickerby had really vivid straw-yellow hair and a ginger moustache. He was very springy and bouncy, quite loud and a very good History teacher. His lessons were very interactive, he would wave his arms, talk dramatically and he would listen to you as well. He would pick everybody at random rather than just picking the people who knew their stuff. He had a laugh, he was the whole package, which was great. There was no grey areas with him, you were either enjoying the lesson or you were out of his lesson.

"Mr Searle, head of Art, never looked any different from the day I started to the day I left. He was a gentleman, lovely guy. I never saw him get angry about anything…

"Mr May was an extremely funny guy and even in Year 7 we were bigger than him, but he was well respected and had a great sense of humour. When he shouted he became ten feet tall. He was vocally big but he would often make fun of himself as well. He was a nice guy.

"Miss Granger, I think because she was older and a lady, was very much a 'Laura Ashley' sort of lady in my mind: tweed skirt, bun, grey hair. She was the real school 'Ma'am' and an extremely good teacher. You don't realise at the time but I think respect begins with how teachers look.

"Mr Grasby taught woodwork and technical drawing. He had clicky segs in his shoes and dressed in a tweed jacket as if he was going shooting. His catchphrase used to be 'What do you think you're doing, BOY?'

"Mrs Frearson looked like she worked on a health farm: well-tanned with vivid pink lipstick. She was an extremely nice lady, very bouncy and always warming up when she was talking to you. She wore a green jog suit always. She was always immaculate and took pride in herself even when wearing casual PE kit. She was an attractive woman and looked after herself but she was actually quite old for her active role.

"Mr Cookson was 'Chinny' because he had an angular jaw - but there was nothing disrespectful about our attitude towards him. He was a good teacher. He taught Science, and could be very vocal and get very, very cross. He took it very seriously in lesson and would go the colour of a traffic light when he was mad: he could be quite scary.

"Miss Harrison and Mr Martin took Rural Studies. If you were naughty in their lesson you had to put on some big brown overalls and then muck out the sheep, pigs or cows."

Julie Hethershaw started teaching at the school in 1976 and she remembered two distinct groups of staff in her early years: "My first impression of the job was that there was not much pressure. The staff all seemed much older than me, but they were friendly and easy-going. People walked out of the staff room at the end of the day and they didn't take any work home. There were smaller class sizes and perhaps lower expectations of pupils. We had a lot more freedom to teach as we wanted... A few keen staff made a great impression on me, particularly Roger May, Bill Roe, Pete Searle (who was madly into fund-raising) and Mick Keeling. Oliver Foreman, who started just before me, was into camping and it wasn't long before I was roped into it because I could drive the minibus and they needed a woman to supervise the girls... (5)

Roger May.

Julie also recalled the impact of the new head: "When Keith Atkinson took up his duties as head teacher in 1978 he made an impression from day one. He was out and about the whole time – and not very keen on paperwork. If anything was going on, he was there."

Julie still teaches at the school at the time of writing and she shared with me her reasons for participating in every aspect of school life for over thirty years: "Although I arrived at Tuxford School almost by accident it has been a major part of my life and I don't regret all the extra time that I have put in over the years. The people I have worked with and the place itself have been very rewarding, but I attribute my personal involvement in a wide range of extra-curricular activities, to coming from a family of 'doers': volunteer types who would never dream of sitting back and thinking it was someone else's

Pete Searle and Dennis Knox.

Mr Atkinson's portrait by one of the students.

job to organise."

An analysis of prior service to Tuxford School by Mr Atkinson's 1978 team of teachers' reveals that ten – roughly 22 percent - had taught there for over ten years. A further five had taught between five and seven years. The rest, 63 percent, had been at the school for four years or less. During my researches for this book an opinion has been expressed to me that Mr Atkinson's first team of teachers was dominated by a high proportion who had taught in the secondary modern for several years and were resistant to raising standards. The figures suggest that this is a myth. However Mr Atkinson's arrival did make a difference.

Mick Keeling summed up the impact of the new head on the staff: "Keith was very good at man management based on making people feel good about themselves. He had a very positive 'can do' approach to everything. Whereas before Tuxford had been a friendly and safe environment with fairly low expectations academically, after Keith's arrival it was a place with unlimited horizons. Keith was a dynamic leader and we couldn't say that about Bunny (Mr Woodward). Bunny was more of a cuddly grandfather."

I am grateful to Mick for the following insight into staff attitudes, the Tuxford culture and the new head's approach to management: "Keith empowered people and let them make mistakes sometimes if they could develop through the experience. If you did make mistakes he was there to catch you. He was not there to kick your ass all over the place, that was not his style. He would reason I'm in charge and the buck stops here: if I let someone do something, I take at least some responsibility for it! Because he talked things through you didn't feel inadequate and you would give it another go. He would never crush someone's spirit. As a result people were eager to make a contribution above and beyond their salary. This really changed the school. In my time here we have not had people saying, 'That isn't part of my job' as you get elsewhere. There has been a blindness to rank and pay scale here and this shows in the humour. I remember when Dennis Knox (Deputy Head) came to school in a very light suit. This was at a time when a popular TV programme was set in the African bush and one character wore a white suit, so all day long Dennis endured people singing the theme tune 'Daktari, Daktari' as he walked past. He never wore that suit to school again. There is a great sense of humour here and most people have learned to laugh at themselves. The same applies to students. We can enjoy a laugh in class at occasional mild practical jokes, if it is based on respect. We have not had much in the way of vindictive malicious behaviour." (1)

Several members of Mr Atkinson's original staff expressed similar sentiments. Dennis Knox, speaking with characteristic modesty, was quick to praise the new man in charge: "Keith had charisma as a leader. He was the sort of fellow that you wanted to work with. Another trait - that I sometimes found annoying - was that he was always blooming well right! More than once at Leadership Team meetings (what we called The Policy Committee in those days) I spoke out against proposals and said that they wouldn't work. He would reply, 'Yes they will, just give them a chance.' And of course they did. I can't remember a single occasion when he was proved wrong. He could always make a good decision." (4) It was not long after he arrived and established his proactive style of management that Mr Atkinson became known simply as 'The Boss' by staff colleagues.

Carol Brumpton remembered his impact on her and the other students: "I was caught smoking by Mr Atkinson once, on the top field in the shot-put area above the tennis court. Someone shouted a warning and I was totally oblivious to it. The next thing he was there, so I put my hand over it and consequently my hand got very hot. I had a massive blister for days. He kicked my foot and said, 'Get down to my office, you' and I was like ooooh - devastated. Events such as this led me to befriend the postman. I would give him a few sweets and a nice smile and say, 'I'm getting a letter from school, can you help me out?' and he would. I didn't get as many letters as I deserved overall!"

As for students in the classroom setting, Julie Hethershaw offered some of her early memories as a teacher of domestic science / home economics / food technology: "There have not been many disasters or breakages in my lessons over the years. Very little food produced in the classroom has been inedible. Several of my former pupils who have been to university have told me that they were the only ones in their halls of residence or bedsits who could cook. However, on one occasion there was a fire drill in the middle of a practical lesson when we were making toffee. Whilst we were outside being counted the toffee set in the pans and it was dreadfully difficult to get it out. I can also remember a boy misunderstanding my instructions when we were preparing a Victoria sandwich cake. He thought he had to put the baking tin in the oven upside down – so his mixture oozed out and was stuck to the bottom of the oven. He didn't have much to take home for his parents!

"The early gas cookers in my teaching area used bottled gas and on one memorable occasion a pupil didn't light his properly. When I went to investigate there was a flash that burnt my eyebrows and singed my hair. I was a bit shocked, but it wasn't a casualty job! Recently a girl in Year 7 confided that it was her father who was the culprit."

Classroom incidents such as these are timeless. Similar events have happened down the years and they will continue to occur in future. However the main event of 1978, the change of leadership, was significant for the school. Tuxford School had changed status two years previously and to some extent its focus had already shifted away from its rural setting, but acceptance of the new role and new focus would take longer. The new headteacher's task was to turn vision into reality. Summing up Mr Atkinson's immediate impact as the school's second headteacher Mick Keeling suggested: "Acko's appointment was exceptionally good news for Tuxford School… He brought a new rush of energy and events became bolder and more ambitious. He was lucky because he had a lot of new staff who were not happy just to come in, do the job and go home."

Sources

1   *Thirty Two Years & Three Headteachers*, Mick Keeling, Tuxford School Archive Papers, unpublished, 2007

2   *New Head for Tuxford school*, Retford Times, 5 May 1978

3   *Tuxford's first Comprehensive Intake*, Carol Brumpton, Tuxford School Archive Papers, unpublished, 2007

4   *A View from Policy Committee*, Dennis Knox, Tuxford School Archive Papers, unpublished, 2007

5   *My Career at Tuxford*, Julie Hethershaw, Tuxford School Archive Papers, unpublished, 2006

Staying on:

The Emergence of Tuxford Sixth Form

We have noted already that the initial scheme to turn Tuxford County Secondary School into a comprehensive included no provision for a sixth form. The proposal, published by the local education authority in the mid 1960s, was that the school should cater for the 11-15 age range only (or 11-16 after the school leaving age was raised). However, the mid 70s scheme - that was implemented - envisaged Tuxford's reorganised school catering for the whole 11 to 18 age range as well as for the full ability range.

Shortage of accommodation was just one of a number of significant challenges faced by the school before the sixth form opened in September 1980. A sixth form block had been promised only "...when viable Sixth Form numbers come through" so no specialist accommodation would be available for the first students. (1) Early sixth form lessons were taught in any convenient space anywhere in the school instead of in rooms where seating layout, additional resources, displays, etc would be more appropriate for the different teaching methods employed post 16. A dedicated sixth form centre would have had better provision for private study, extra-curricular activities, etc but daytime use of the youth centre as a common room was negotiated with the county leisure services department as an adequate interim solution.

Lack of money in the school budget for development was another challenge. The government of prime minister Margaret Thatcher was seeking to cut expenditure in the public sector and county, which administered the delegated education budget, had to ensure that its schools were run efficiently. Over-capacity was a concern within Nottinghamshire as there were fewer young people of secondary school age in the county. (Falling rolls was, in fact, an issue nationwide after the post-war "baby boomers" had worked their way through the education system and many women of that generation chose to work for longer and start families later). A reduced budget for Tuxford School had already led to a cut in general allowance (the money that could be spent on books, stationery, etc) and further economies had to be made wherever possible. The school was told, towards the end of 1978/79, that it also had to lose a member of staff due to financial cutbacks – preferably through early retirement. (Tom Grasby, one of the original staff, retired at the end of the summer term of 1979). Mr Atkinson wrote to the Director of Education during the term to make a case for special treatment of Tuxford School in its build up to post 16 provision, but little was forthcoming. A small grant was received in 1980 for post 16 Maths and Science development.

Introduction of the sixth form inevitably made disproportionate demands on both teaching staff time and resources during the 1980/81 financial year. Text books had to be purchased, staff had to attend exam board meetings or the new courses simply could not run. Of course, on the positive side, post 16 students brought in additional revenue to compensate, at least partially, for any drop in numbers lower down the school.

The fear of falling numbers lasted for approximately ten years (until schools took responsibility for their own budgets). As it turned out, a fairly dramatic loss of students occurred between 1987 and 1992, but staff jobs had already been lost after 1980 as the budget dictated. Mr Atkinson wrote to governors in April 1979: "...our Primary feeder schools suggest an intake of less than 150 in September, leaving spare capacity in both upper and lower schools. There is

Reproduced courtesy of *the Retford Times*. 25 Jan 1985.

a clear pattern emerging with prospective pupils from Norwell and Sutton-on-Trent moving towards Newark and from Walesby and Kirton to move towards Tuxford. Perhaps there is a case for re-drawing of boundaries? In any case the Governing Body ought to look favourably upon applications from outside our catchment area otherwise our roll will begin a slow decline." (2) As time passed the loss of in-catchment students to Newark schools diminished. Parents from Norwell and Sutton-on-Trent – and other areas - were increasingly impressed by the school's provision for more able students and the establishment of a successful sixth form would impress them further.

Opening the sixth form a year before the first comprehensive intake was able to join it was a third challenge. Although

OXFORD BOUND — Eighteen-year-old Chris Hogg, a pupil at Tuxford Comprehensive School, has accepted a place at Queen's College, Oxford, to read Mathematics. Chris plays soccer for Tuxford's highly successful U19 side and hopes to continue playing whilst at University. The Sixth Form at Tuxford was set up in 1982 following reorganisation in 1976. As well as traditional 'A' Level courses pupils are able to follow City & Guilds Foundation Courses. Adults have also joined the Sixth Form. "We hope to have more parents and friends working alongside the pupils next year," said Headmaster Mr Keith Atkinson, "That's what Community Education is all about."

Pedal power helps the elderly

The leg-weary cyclists after their marathon ride. From left to right: teacher Chris Bray, Chris Johnson, Louise Cartledge, Joanne Allwood, Alison Rogers, Sarah Priestley, Daryl Whetton, Elizabeth Gorst, Nigel Pickard and Mrs Frearson. Photo ref: B1668.

SIXTH formers from Tuxford Comprehensive School got on their bikes and took to the road for an 82-mile sponsored ride on Sunday.

The eight pupils, accompanied by two teachers and a former pupil, were raising money for the school's Sixth Form Community Club whose members help out elderly people in need. The route was round the 30

The riders set off at 5.30 in the morning from Askham, where they had spent the night at the home of games teacher Eunice Frearson.

Not being experienced cyclists most of them pedalled for a 10-mile stint and then took a rest in the balloon-bedecked mini bus which accompanied the ride all the way.

But two of the cyclists, Nigel Pickard and ex-pupil Dale Fields made the complete ride,

ahead of the main field.

On the way there were burst tyres, a wheel fell off one of the bikes and the youngsters rescued a lamb which was tangled up in a nylon fence. And at the end of the ride there were 11 pairs of very tired legs after pedalling at least 25 miles each.

Said Mrs Frearson, who organised the event: 'It was fantastic, we really had a great time."

It isn't yet known how much has been raised but when all the money has come in it will go towards providing an old age

the mini bus which takes community Club members to do jobs for old people.

Another project the club is planning is a "talking newspaper" for the local community using audio tape.

Reproduced courtesy of the *Retford Times*. Date unknown.

twenty students from the final secondary modern cohort had expressed an interest in staying on into the sixth form during Spring 1980, just eleven were registered in the following January, one term after it had opened. Nevertheless, the list of subjects taught is impressive for such small numbers: Maths, English, History, Biology, Chemistry, Physics, Art and Economics. (3) The disadvantage of beginning courses early was that end-of-course examination successes would be modest, but the advantage was that staff could become thoroughly acquainted with syllabuses and texts before class sizes became larger. Long-serving deputy headteacher "Jeff" Jeffcott had opposed the move according to a colleague who told me, off the record: "I remember Jeffcott saying, 'No student at Tuxford is capable of A' level in anything, so why are we bothering?' "

The person charged with guiding the school's first Advanced Level students - responsible for establishing a workable study routine - was Head of Sixth Form Mrs Val Brock, a teacher of English. (Another of her roles was developing the education of 'gifted and talented' children throughout the school). During the first year she could guide the students personally as they were few in number and she got to know them well, so she was disappointed to be absent from school, following an operation, for most of the 1982 summer term when those remaining were sitting their exams. Head of History Chris Bray and Maths teacher Mick Keeling took over her pastoral duties for the term.

During its second year the sixth form grew to 42 in number, most of whom were in the lower sixth. Other staff became involved in organising activities for the post 16 students. Chris Bray encouraged students to start a school magazine, Tremor. At least four intelligent, lively and well-written editions were produced by the 1981 cohort of sixth formers, but when Mr Bray left the staff at the end of 1984 the publication disappeared with him apart from a brief revival in 1989. Chris Bray also supported another venture, the sixth form community club, organised principally by PE teacher Eunice Frearson. The two of them led the club on a Sunday sponsored cycle ride through the school's catchment area during summer term 1983, starting at 5.30 in the morning. Student Nigel Pickard and former student Dale Shields completed the whole 82 mile route, but most of the group rode twenty five miles only and covered the rest of the route in the minibus. Pictured in the Retford Times behind the club banner with the two teachers and Nigel were Chris Johnson, Louise Cartledge, Joanne Allwood, Alison Rogers, Sarah Priestley, Daryl Whetton and Elizabeth Gorst. An earlier venture by the club was a Christmas party for local pensioners attended by more than one hundred.

Facilities for sixth formers slowly improved during Mrs Brock's stewardship. A specialist sixth form science laboratory was created in 1981 by converting Room 7. (It later became known as Science 3). In 1982 two teaching spaces were created in the tower block for sixth form classes: an English and Modern Language room on the top floor in what became known as 1A and a Geography and History room on the first floor, 4A. At the same time a fume cupboard was installed in the sixth form science laboratory.

Top Marks

TUXFORD pupil Mark Huson has accepted a place at Balliol College, Oxford to read Modern History, starting in October.

Mark, whose parents live in Lexington Gardens, Tuxford, did so well in the entrance examinations he was offered a place unconditionally.

Mr Keith Atkinson, Headmaster of Tuxford Comprehensive said he was deighted with the news, especially since Mark had broken new ground by being the school's first pupil to go to Oxford to read an arts subject. His success was a great boost to all his teachers, said Mr Atkinson.

Reproduced courtesy of the *Retford Times*. 12 Jan 1987.

90

The curriculum also developed when one year City and Guilds foundation courses were introduced in 1982. It was felt that this development would be welcomed by local young people who had difficulty attending FE colleges due to transport difficulties. The staffing level for the year was set at 47.5 by county, an increase of one, so Mr Atkinson announced that the priority would be to appoint someone to facilitate the setting up of 16-19 courses. Dave Cook was appointed and it was he who organised the one year courses.

The school's second cohort of sixth formers, members of the 1976 full ability intake, sat their A' Level examinations in May and June 1983. Subsequently, Mr Atkinson proudly informed the school's governing body in September that the students listed below had won places on degree courses and were, therefore "…the school's first direct university entrants": (3)

Name	Higher Education destination	Degree course
Teresa Harlow	UMIST (Manchester)	Town & Country Planning
Jane Foster	University of Hull	History
John Foster	University of Salford	Chemical Engineering
Suzanne Hope	Newcastle University	Plant Science
Joanne Love	Newcastle Polytechnic	Chemistry
Helen Storer	Middlesex Polytechnic	Graphics

The Newark Advertiser reported a year later, on 28 September 1984, that two former Tuxford students had won prizes in their first year in university: "Jane Foster, 19, of Trent Lane, North Clifton, has been awarded a history prize at Hull, and Teresa Harlow, 19, of Main Street, Laneham, became the top first year student at Manchester, where she is studying town and country planning." (4)

When Mrs Brock left in April 1984 to become deputy head of Alderman White School she was succeeded as Head of Sixth Form by Warren Cookson, head of science and leader of the short-lived Science, Maths and Business Studies faculty. Thirty per cent of the fifth year students stayed on in September to joined the sixth form: a much better figure than the Bassetlaw average of sixteen percent.

Mr Cookson was very interested in providing sixth formers with an insight into government and democracy as part of the General Studies course. The Retford Times of 5th October 1984 recorded the visit of five Bassetlaw District councillors and four council officers for questioning by students: "The sixth-formers will go to their local parish council meeting soon, and a district council meeting to see local democracy in action." Mr Cookson explained that he hoped the visit would help students to learn a skill also: "We are trying to give more confidence to pupils who leave this school to take the floor at large meetings." (5)

In January 1985 the school proudly announced the news that Chris Hogg of Harby would be the first Tuxford student to gain a place at Oxford. The Retford Times carried the news that he had accepted a place at Queen's College to read Mathematics. (6) (The school's press release misleadingly claimed that the sixth form had been opened in 1982 and, unfortunately, the news story repeated this).

In March the sixth form was in the news again because it held a formal debate attended by representatives of Retford schools. The motion was: This house is in favour of unilateral nuclear disarmament. A CND Council member spoke in favour of the motion and was supported by Stephanie Gorst; a representative of Peace through NATO spoke against as did Jason Rawding. The debate was described as "somewhat heated" before the motion was convincingly defeated. (7)

Warren Cookson's leadership of the sixth form lasted just over two years because he left at the end of the 1985/86 academic year. Headteacher Keith Atkinson decided not to replace him with one person, but with a team of three. Mick Keeling, one of the three, recalled how his appointment came about: "When I was appointed Joint Head of Sixth Form with Freddie White and Dave Cook it was at a time when 'collegiality' was the buzz word in education. I think Acko was looking for something more than the three of us as individuals could provide but it meant that he could only provide a modest salary compared to the higher scale earned by a single Head of Sixth in other schools. (We were on Scale 3 whereas a typical Head of Sixth would be on Scale 5). Freddie was keen to accept the arrangement and said to us, 'We can make this work. Mick has been working on Higher Education links for a long time so he can focus on that, Dave has been promoting one year courses, so he can focus on that and I can focus on areas that interest me.' We agreed to give it a go and soon we were having differences and duplicating effort but we made it work well in the end. In fact I took the job without any pay increase at all because I was already on a 3. I gave up my role as second in Maths and moved across whereas the other two had a salary increase." (8)

Weeks after the new management team was appointed the whole future of the sixth form was in doubt. The local education authority published a policy consultation leaflet in October asking for comments on a draft proposal to abolish school sixth forms and to replace them with larger tertiary colleges which could offer a wider choice of subjects, be more efficient in terms of staffing costs and possibly increase the number of students opting for post 16 education. Most schools opposed the plan as it would force students to travel further and would attract several of their more able staff to seek new opportunities elsewhere. Tuxford School had waited a long time to establish a sixth form and it wasn't going to give it up without a fight. Keith Atkinson enlisted governors, staff, parents, the local community and former students to the cause. With his encouragement they responded to the consultation invitation with determination. Local parish councils passed resolutions opposing the plan and the Newark Advertiser of 16 January 1987 reported that a petition organised by former students had been delivered to County Hall. (9) The county council had promised to publish its development plan in March, but this was postponed until July. When July came the plan was quietly dropped. The government had

More voices against 6th form abolition

Former Tuxford Comprehensive School students have added their weight to objections by governors to recommendations from **Nottinghamshire Education** Authority to abolish sixth-forms and establish tertiary colleges.

Headmaster, Mr Keith Atkinson, said one student, currently doing research at Manchester University, considered that urban located tertiary colleges would discriminate against isolated communities such as Tuxford.

She also thought bus deregulation would exacerbate the situation and accelerate rural decline, increasing the drift to the towns.

The student said she and many of her friends attended Tuxford Comprehensive School because there was no realistic alternative. She had recently graduated, said Mr. Atkinson.

He emphasised the strength of support former pupils had for the School, saying the recent sixth-form re-union party attracted 200 students and staff.

"I think it is quite remarkable that after only five years so many returned at such a busy time of the year," he said. "It shows the great support we have for what is now the fastest growing sixth-form in Nottinghamshire."

The event was organised by Mr. Freddie White who said the re-union was so successful it had established itself as an annual party.

The present sixth-form, under the leadership of Miss Julie Heathershaw, provided a buffet and disco

Reproduced courtesy of *North Notts Guardian*. 21 Jan 1987.

Head set against opting out

RUMOURS that Tuxford Comprehensive School is going to opt out of the county system and be supported directly by the Government have been quashed by headmaster Mr Keith Atkinson.

He told the Advertiser: "In view of the academic, sporting, artistic and social success here I can understand people assuming that we might wish to go independent under the terms of the new Education Bill.

"But we are more than satisfied with the service provided by Nottinghamshire County Council and would not wish to sever our connection. The decision is really up to the governors and parents — but my advice is stay with the county."

Mr Atkinson said there was an automatic assumption that successful schools meant independent schools. "I am against this because I consider Nottinghamshire County Council delivers a good service and keeps us very well funded. Despite cutbacks, we have a developing curriculum here."

Governors' chairman Mr Jim Kitchen said the matter had not been discussed by his members and the item was not on the agenda for the next governors' meeting on Monday, although the matter could come up informally.

"The rumour may have come from a parents' and Governors' meeting in the summer," he said. "I would suspect if anyone is going to see a school as going independent through the Bill, they would probably look at Tuxford because of its growing reputation."

Newark solicitor Mr Kitchen, who has two children at the school, said he echoed Mr Atkinson's views. "I cannot think there would be any strong feeling from the governors' body to go independent but I cannot speak for the parents who may be the body to take such a decision when more details are known."

Reproduced courtesy of the *Newark Advertiser.* 18 Sept 1987.

announced plans to allow schools to opt out of county control – and the proposed reorganisation of sixth forms might have provoked some Nottinghamshire schools to do so. (10)

A second Tuxford student won a place at Oxford University in February. The Retford Times reported that Mark Huson of Lexington Gardens, Tuxford would be reading Modern History at Balliol College from October. (11) By now there were 72 students in the sixth form at Tuxford and the additional accommodation promised by county twelve years before had failed to materialise. After seven years the sixth form was well established in spite of the relatively poor conditions in which it operated.

Sources

1   *Plans for Comprehensive Education…*, Retford Times, 3 January 1975

2   *Headteacher's Report to Governing Body April 1979*, Keith Atkinson, Tuxford School Archive Papers, unpublished

3   *Headteacher's Report to Governing Body September 1980*, Keith Atkinson, Tuxford School Archive Papers, unpublished

4   *Top student*, Newark Advertiser, 28 September 1984

5   *Pupils focus on councils*, Retford Times, 5 October 1984

6   *Oxford bound*, Retford Times, 25 January 1985

7   *Thumbs down to CND*, Retford Times, 29 March 1985

8   *Thirty Two Years & Three Headteachers*, Mick Keeling, Tuxford School Archive Papers, unpublished, 2007

9   *Plans upset ex-pupils*, Newark Advertiser, 16 January 1987

10   *Colleges plan is shelved*, Newark Advertiser, 24 July 1987

11   *Top Marks*, Retford Times, 12 February 1987

Legislation and Regulation 1986-92

"Just one damn thing after another" was headteacher Keith Atkinson's dismissive summary of Thatcher government education reforms in the late 1980s. (1) He wasn't necessarily opposed to the changes, but he believed that they were being introduced too rapidly and without adequate funding. To place the words in context, we need to know that teachers throughout the country felt little goodwill towards the government or local authorities in 1988 because they had been engaged in a bitter and protracted pay dispute with employers a few years before. Nevertheless, the reforms went ahead and their impact on Tuxford School was profound.

Mr Atkinson reported to governors in May 1984: "Spring Term was long and was disrupted by snow in January and an industrial dispute in April... One cloud on the horizon is a possible dispute between teacher unions and the Authorities as a result of the failure to take pay talks to arbitration. As we have seen before, rural schools suffer very badly in such circumstances." (2) There had already been disruption to schools in spring 1982 through union action. Teachers felt aggrieved that their pay was falling behind that of other professions and that they were not rewarded for the many hours of work performed out of school on planning, preparation, assessment, etc. In dispute with employers they used the vagueness of their contracts as a powerful weapon because they could disrupt normal school life by "withdrawal of goodwill": no more report writing at home, no parent evenings, no out of hours sports fixtures or trips. Mrs Thatcher, famously, was very happy to "take on" trade unions and was determined not to give in to pressure so the dispute dragged on sporadically. In his September 1985 report to governors Mr Atkinson expressed his concerns: "...the teachers' dispute and industrial action rambles on and the prospect of increasing disruption comes ever nearer. I am not confident that 85/86 will bring peace in the schools... The annual programme of camps was completed satisfactorily. Visits took place to Sheffield and London... The continuing dispute is cause for concern not because of the quality of teaching but rather the lack of time spent on planning for new curriculum initiative. The effect on the new GCSE, due to be examined in 1988, could be catastrophic – some teacher associations are already withdrawing from development work. It is sad to report that no cricket matches took place during the (summer) term and no soccer, hockey or netball fixtures are planned this term". (3)

In July 1985 the NASUWT (the union that represented most Tuxford staff) decided to

increase pressure by calling for members to take strike action in October. By instructing groups of members to absent themselves for about thirty minutes each on a particular day (instead of calling an all out strike) classes could be disrupted day after day with little impact on members' pay. Director of Education John Fox wrote to all Nottinghamshire teachers on 29th November to inform them that a special sub committee had met to consider the "guerrilla style" strike action. The committee had decided that teachers would lose

Keith Atkinson wanted students to enjoy a varied programme of extra-curricular activities.

94

a half day's pay for every session they missed. (4) Mr Atkinson's next report on the effects of the dispute was published in February1986: "Since September last no extra-curricular activities have taken place at Tuxford School. Industrial Action has severely disrupted the normal work at Tuxford on nine separate occasions. Meals continued to be served in that there were sufficient staff on site to provide cover." He was concerned that students would react badly to the absence of a full programme of extra-curricular activities: that Tuxford wouldn't be the exciting and fun place that it had been for many years. (5) However he had better news in May: "Spring Term 1986 saw the official end of a year of disruption of schools... The situation at present was well expressed by our Chairman (parent and local solicitor Jim Kitchen) as 'a Mexican Standoff'... Some teachers have restored goodwill, most are resentful." Unfortunately the union action continued in Nottinghamshire "...due to the intransigence of the Local Authority in their refusal to rescind the letter of February 12th 1985." (6) He was optimistic that in spite of the continuing dispute with county the school could get back to normal – and indeed his September report showed that his optimism had been justified: "Alone amongst the Nottinghamshire schools Tuxford put on a full programme of social and sporting events (in the summer term) and all programmed parents evenings and report sessions were honoured. After the poor treatment at the hands of the Government and the County, Tuxford staff deserve great credit for what they achieved. I certainly felt that the Term was the most pleasant one I had spent in teaching over the past 25 years." (7)

The government responded to the prolonged dispute by passing the Teachers' Pay and Conditions Act 1987. This changed conditions of service so that in future work performed by teachers outside school hours was contractual, not merely a goodwill gesture. The Order under the Act confirmed that teachers would work a minimum of 1265 hours per year. There would be 190 teaching days in the year and five others for use as specified by employers. Subparagraph f of the Order specified that after 1st August 1987 "a teacher shall... work such additional hours as may be needed to enable him to discharge effectively his professional duties, including, in particular the marking of pupils' work, the writing of reports on pupils and the preparation of lessons, teaching material and teaching programmes. The amount of time required for this purpose beyond the 1265 hours referred to... shall not be defined by the employer but shall depend upon the work needed to discharge the teacher's duties..." (8) In passing this measure the government ensured that unions would be unable to employ their very effective "guerrilla style" tactics again.

Many schools, under the direction of county, responded to the 1265 hours requirement by setting a "time budget." Keith Atkinson had little patience for such exercises. The measure was intended to make it clear to reluctant teachers that they must attend meetings and training sessions, but the Tuxford head was convinced that his staff required no coercion. He made it clear that he would not bother with the requirement. The tensions experienced in other schools were avoided and the reputation of "The Boss" was further enhanced.

At first the introduction of five additional (non teaching) working days was regarded as an imposition by the profession but the value of the days was quickly recognised. It was intended that they should be used for in-service training and throughout the profession they became known as "Baker days" after the Secretary of State for Education of the time, Kenneth Baker.

A fundamental tenet of government policy-making during the Thatcher years was to promote the working of market forces in all sectors of the economy. In education the intention was to offer parents a genuine choice of schools for their child: making available to them different types of education provider including independent schools, specialist schools and selective schools. The government believed the only way of achieving this was to reduce the power of local education authorities because LEAs were essentially planners and regulators interfering in "markets." They aimed to regulate education within their areas, to raise standards across the board, to distribute resources wisely and fairly; unfortunately regulation tends to support the weak and fails to reward the best because a standardised "product" is promoted so that is why local authorities at the time could be viewed as opponents of competition. The role of LEAs on school governing bodies was an early target for reform. The Education (No. 2) Act of 1986 introduced equal representation for parents and the LEA on school governing bodies and defined the composition of governing bodies according to size. (Schools with more than 600 pupils were entitled to five parent governors). In effect this Act removed LEA control over governor decision-making and gave parents (and the headteacher) greater power to influence decisions in schools. The Act required governors to issue an Annual Report to all parents and to call an Annual Meeting of parents to discuss the report. Another change introduced by the Act was that it gave headteachers rather than LEAs control of the curriculum.

Previous chairmen of governors such as Mr S Snowden Housley and Mr Cecil Hempsall had been councillors and council-nominated, but since the 1986 Act the chairmen have been parents including the one at the time of writing, Mr Mick Jones of East Markham. Annual meetings throughout the country were never well attended and have since been discontinued, but early Tuxford meetings attracted a few parents. The annual reports

'GCSE credit must go to teachers'

A HEADMASTER has praised teachers for their work in achieving good results in the first GCSE examinations.

Mr Keith Atkinson, headmaster of Tuxford School, Newark, said that before politicians began to make "outrageous claims" for what they have achieved, praise should go to the teachers.

He said: "It is the classroom teacher who has delivered these results.

"A new exam introduced into schools in the teeth of a dispute-

without sufficient resources, often without even a syllabus and dogged by bad publicity could have been a major disaster.

"Instead it is a great success. Standards have been significantly raised and overall pupil achievement is up.

"All credit to the classroom teacher who got on and did a thoroughly professional job and at the same time saved Kenneth Baker's reputation.

"I hope he has the good sense to tell them so," Mr Atkinson added.

Reproduced courtesy of the *Nottingham Evening Post*. 7 Oct 1988.

PUT YOUR BEST FOOT FORWARD

Pictured here are Tuxford Comprehensive School pupils on a 10 mile sponsored "WACKY WALK".
They are heading for a secret destination - High Marnham Power Station. The walk is the final event in the quest for a new mini-bus.
June 1987.

to parents were useful in promoting the work of the governors and in summarising the achievements of the school.

The next government educational initiative was to pass the most important piece of legislation affecting schools since 1944: the Education Reform Act of July 1988. Two of its provisions further shifted power from LEAs to parents. Under the first of these parents were able to decide by vote whether a school should seek grant-maintained (GM) status, making it independent of the LEA. Although several schools in Lincolnshire voted in favour of independence as there were tempting financial incentives, few schools in Nottinghamshire chose to opt out of LEA control but, as we have seen already, the possibility of a vote saved county sixth forms. Keith Atkinson, interviewed for the 18 September 1987 edition of the Newark Advertiser, denied rumours that he was considering grant maintained status for Tuxford: "…we are more than satisfied with the service provided by Nottinghamshire County Council and would not wish to sever our connection." (9)

The second provision of the Act greatly increased the responsibility of headteachers and governors by introducing local management of schools (LMS) from 1990: the delegation of budget control to individual schools and budget allocation based on numbers of students on roll rather than on perceived operational needs. Successful schools such as Tuxford would gain under this system whereas schools unable to attract sufficient students would see their budgets shrink. Deputy headteacher Dennis Knox was responsible for the budget and he welcomed the reform as it enabled him to spend money on overdue improvements: "I was managing the school finances at a time of relative generosity by government. I was prudent and I always ensured that I was in control of the budget, but I was able to make big improvement within the school such as getting it painted throughout for the first time in years. We also replaced many of the pupils' chairs." (10) However the headteacher was concerned about the possible impact on the fabric of the building. He told governors in January 1990: "In general terms the condition of the school can only be said to be 'fair'. As LMS approaches it is clear that the Authority is only in a position to deal with emergencies. A site audit must be carried out before responsibility is off-loaded onto the Governing Body." (11)

Major capital investment aside, LMS enabled schools to be more creative in setting budgets. They could make savings in some areas to increase spending in others whereas before their freedom to vire funds had been restricted. Of course the increased responsibility to manage funds in school created extra work for office staff. Mr Knox explained how he relied on his team of clerical assistants: "When county changed to computer accounting I became reliant on Joyce, Mollie and Pauline to manage the system, but I always kept my paper balance sheet." At first county retained a small proportion of each school's money (still a significant sum) to cover its own administration expenses, but later the government tightened the rules to stop this. A few years after the start of local management Tuxford became a "cheque book school" which freed it from restrictions on when the budget could be spent: instead of the budget allocation sitting in the LEA bank account until released in monthly tranches it could now be paid into a school account and the school could gain any interest. The sums involved were large from the start. The allocation for 1992/93 was over one and a half million pounds, for example, most of which was committed to staff salaries. Roger Longden took over responsibility for the budget in 1994 and was assisted by Mollie Whitehead from the school office. Much of the clerical workload that transferred to the school from county following the introduction of Local Management of Schools was (and still is at the time of writing) undertaken by Pauline Merrills and Liz Boneham.

Although the two provisions discussed already were significant changes, the July 1988 Act will probably be best remembered for establishing a prescribed 'national curriculum' of nine foundation subjects for all maintained primary schools with an additional one, modern languages, for secondary pupils. In future – to be phased in before 1992 - a pupil's progress would be monitored through four 'key stages' and so year group titles were standardised throughout the different key stages from year one in infants to year thirteen in the upper sixth form. Ten levels of attainment were introduced for assessment of each subject; detailed programmes of study were introduced by Department of Education and Science regulations. Standard assessment tasks at the end of each key stage would not only enable the progress of an individual child to be tracked but also would provide performance data on each school and enable schools to be compared. Introduction of General Certificate of Secondary Education courses for fourth year students in 1986 (to replace O' Level and C.S.E.) had involved staff in a great deal of work. New syllabuses and a different grading system had to be mastered, but also G.C.S.E. had a greater proportion of coursework to be marked and moderated. Now, in 1988, when the first candidates were completing their courses the staff faced the prospect of introducing a new curriculum and new tests for younger students too. This would be a massive undertaking involving hours of meetings, thousands of words to assimilate and the devising of new record-keeping systems within departments.

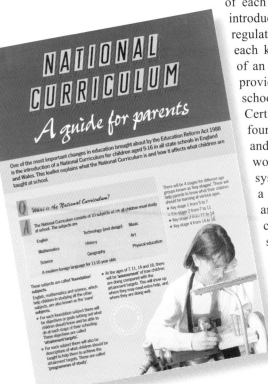

Allocation of sufficient time to the

On Task, On Target *The story of the first fifty years of Tuxford School*

prescribed subjects had to be achieved in schools so timetables would have to be rewritten. Policy Committee took the decision that link courses for older students at Newark Technical College would have to end as students had to concentrate on prescribed subjects. Some subjects taught at Tuxford, such as Drama and Rural Studies, were also outside the national curriculum. The future of the farm unit was reviewed and the decision to phase it out from 1992 was taken reluctantly. Resident stockman David Whitehead was appointed as assistant caretaker. Deputy headteacher Bob Taylor consulted staff about lesson times and proposed introducing thirty teaching periods per week in place of the previous twenty periods to distribute time to subjects more efficiently. This was adopted by Policy Committee in January 1989 to be introduced from September.

In January 1991 Keith Atkinson made governors aware of his opinion of the cost of implementing the national curriculum: "The national curriculum is largely in place for Key Stage 3 pupils. Mr Parker and Departmental Staff are hard at work putting recording and monitoring structures in place. Governors should be aware that despite all Government protestations the vast sums of money spent on implementing the '88 Act do not directly reach the pupil in the classroom. Secondly, staff spent a great deal of time planning ahead only to have their work negated by yet another new bright idea." (12) Writing two years later his views had not altered: "Feedback on the trial SATs (Standard Assessment Tasks) taken last summer in Science and Maths was given to year 10 parents by Mrs Powell and Mrs Fleetwood. Some of the statistics generated are as abstruse as the much vaunted exam League Tables – suffice it to say that in both cases Tuxford was above County and National averages. The huge sums of money spent on both could be better used in schools." (13)

Another government education reform of this period – and the last one to be discussed

A sixth-former and a history teacher have located memorials to their great-uncles in an emotional school trip to World War One battlefields.

Rebecca Hemslock and Mr. Freddie White think their relatives may have known each other as they were both serving in the King's Royal Rifle Corps when they died in "Devil's Wood" on the Somme in August 1916, within days of each other.

The two were among 41 pupils and four teachers from Tuxford Comprehensive School who toured The Somme and Ypres, Belgium during half term, discovering two live grenades and other ammunition.

Now Mr. White wants to talk with World War One survivors in Tuxford and Retford areas.

Somme battlefield reminders were brought back by Tuxford School pupils after a school visit. Showing off their finds with teachers Freddie White, Rhona Ward and Linda Hibbard are Simon Drury and Chris Coulson, and Rob Over. Nov 1986.

here – was the establishment of the Office for Standards in Education (Ofsted) under the Education (Schools) Act 1992. All schools were to be inspected every four years and the inspection findings were to be published for all to see. This would provide parents with valuable information when choosing a school and the government would have reliable judgements on every school in the country for the first time. (Once again this could be seen as a reduction in the role of LEAs because they had previously been responsible for vetting standards in the schools under their control). The first inspection of Tuxford School by an Ofsted team occurred during the week beginning 2 October 1995. Mr Atkinson was already ill by this time so deputy head Beth Soule took on the role of liaising with the inspection team led by Mr Mervyn Griffiths. Boxes of evidence had to be collected by staff prior to the inspection and the inspection programme was very busy so the whole process proved to be exhausting for staff: "The team consisted of 14 inspectors. During the week 243 lessons, 31 tutorial/registration sessions, nine assemblies and a range of extra-curricular activities were inspected… Over 50 planned discussions were held with members of staff and representatives of the governing body." (14)

The changes to Tuxford School brought about by government reforms between 1986 and 1992 were profound. The way the school was governed and financed changed, the programmes of study in all subject areas were revised, new tests and inspection requirements were introduced. As a package the reforms were as important, if not more important, than the school's reorganisation as a comprehensive in 1976. Mr Atkinson praised his staff at every opportunity for rising to the challenge of such rapid change.

Sources

1   *Headteacher's Report to Governing Body April 1988*, Keith Atkinson, Tuxford School Archive Papers, unpublished

2   *Headteacher's Report to Governing Body May 1984*, Keith Atkinson, Tuxford School Archive Papers, unpublished

3   *Headteacher's Report to Governing Body September 1985*, Keith Atkinson, Tuxford School Archive Papers, unpublished

4   *Letter from Director to all Notts teaching staff 29 November 1985*, A.J. Fox, Tuxford School Archive Papers, unpublished

5   *Headteacher's Report to Governing Body February 1986,* Keith Atkinson, Tuxford School Archive Papers, unpublished

6   *Headteacher's Report to Governing Body May 1986*, Keith Atkinson, Tuxford School Archive Papers, unpublished

7   *Headteacher's Report to Governing Body September 1986*, Keith Atkinson, Tuxford School Archive Papers, unpublished

8   *The Education (School Teachers' Pay and Conditions of Employment) Order 1987*, Schedule 3, Section 4.1, DfES, published on internet

9   *Head set against opting out,* Newark Advertiser, 18 September 1987

10   *A View from Policy Committee*, Dennis Knox, Tuxford School Archive Papers, unpublished, 2007

11   *Headteacher's Report to Governing Body January 1990*, Keith Atkinson, Tuxford School Archive Papers, unpublished

12   *Headteacher's Report to Governing Body January 1991,* Keith Atkinson, Tuxford School Archive Papers, unpublished

13   *Headteacher's Report to Governing Body January 1993*, Keith Atkinson, Tuxford School Archive Papers, unpublished

14   *Inspection report on Tuxford School 10 November 1995*, MW Griffiths, Ofsted

Log book 29 Jan 1976: "*D. Ives, P. Searle visit to Spilsby to inspect minibus available for purchase.*"

Log book 4 Mar 1976: "*Minibus broke down on sketching expedition with Mr Searle. Mr Ives to rescue. Arrived in school 5.30. Pupils taken home by car.*"

TUXFORD COMPREHENSIVE SCHOOL
MINI-BUS NEWS
OCTOBER 1987.

SUN INN CHARITY HELP TUXFORD SCHOOL

A cheque for £250 was presented to Tuxford Comprehensive School towards their new mini-bus. The mini-bus is used, not only, for the school, but other Tuxford groups - St.Nicolas Sunday School youth group, Tuxford Senior Citizens and Tuxford Primary School to name a few. May 1987

Chickens wander in teachers' carpark

Mr Keith Atkinson

NINE years ago, Tuxford Secondary School, in common with schools throughout the country, faced the challenge of comprehensive education, which united grammar and secondary modern schools.

The school — now called Tuxford Comprehensive School — was built in 1958. It has more than met the challenge, according to headmaster Mr Keith Atkinson.

"Ten years ago this school was very much the poor relation," he told the Advertiser. "Now we have so many people applying for places that we have to turn potential pupils away."

The school's planned admission limit is 150 pupils per year and this year 147 primary school pupils are automatically entitled to places because they live in the catchment area.

That area is one of the largest in the county, stretching to Elkesley, Harby and Norwell.

There are parents who live outside the catchment area who want to send their children to the school. This year there is room for only three such pupils.

Problems

Priority is given to those with family connections and those who live closest to the school.

The rural nature of the school's area brings logistical problems.

There are 860 pupils and 500 of these are taken in by buses. In some of the remoter villages, parents have banded together to organise voluntary transport groups.

The school is attempting to raise £10,000 for a minibus. The appeal has so far topped £7,000.

Said Mr Atkinson: "I regard this venture as a fine illustration of the strength of Tuxford school.

"Staff, pupils, parents and friends of the school have rallied round to provide this minibus, which is much needed in an isolated rural comprehensive."

Mr Atkinson became head teacher six years ago and the atmosphere prevalent throughout the school must be due to a large extent to his style of management.

A quick tour of the school revealed no sign of vandalism or graffiti, which is characteristic of some secondary schools.

"I'm not saying that we never get any vandalism, but when it occurs, we make stringent efforts to find the culprit," said Mr Atkinson.

Punishments are traditional — lines and detention. The biggest threat is the withdrawal of privileges, such as sport, discos and foreign visits.

A visit to Dallas last year proved a great success and many Americans will be visiting the school on an exchange trip later this year.

Higher

Last year, the school had a 100% pass rate in O-level history and art, and of the 60 pupils who took O-level maths, 93% passed.

Candidates pass an average of 3.4 O-level subjects, significantly higher than the national average.

The school has a thriving sixth form of about 60 youngsters and a staying-on rate of about 28%, compared with the Bassetlaw average of 18%.

Mr Atkinson has no doubts about where the strengths of the school lie — "We have excellent staff. Pupils have a pride in the school. We have a good parent-teacher association and some parents take part in lessons."

School uniform is still worn, although Mr Atkinson prefers to call it school dress — "We are conservative on uniform, although sixth formers don't have to wear it."

"We try to be humorous and informal, but at the same time purposeful."

No one could accuse the school of being traditional and staid.

Unmolested

Morning assembly is just as likely to include verses from pop groups as school hymns and sombre prayers.

Chickens from the school's agricultural department stroll unmolested in the teachers' carpark.

Recently, the school received an EEC rebate of about £250 on its sheep.

Mr Atkinson is considering setting up pupils' councils to involve the youngsters in the running of the school.

Two headmasters from Newark who visited Tuxford school suggested the idea of pupils' councils.

"We are always willing to listen to any suggestions for improving the school," said Mr Atkinson.

"What is exciting about Tuxford is that there is still room for improvement. Parents clearly like what we are doing and I confidently predict continuing improvement."

Reproduced courtesy of the Newark Advertiser. *22 March 1985.*

Computers for the children

INFORMATION technology is being made available for all the pupils at Tuxford School thanks to the formation of a computer suite.

Youngsters are pictured working in the suite, which was opened last month by chairman of the governors Mr Jim Kitchen.

Information technology co-ordinator for the school Mr David Ives said the suite had been created in two months out of three rooms formerly used by the art and craft department which is now housed elsewhere in the school.

One room houses the old technology machines and another room houses the new technology machines for timetabled lessons.

The third room is a computer resource for use by pupils whenever they need it and a data transmission cable has been fed into many of the classrooms so that computers can be moved into other rooms.

Both the old and new machines belong to the Acorn family and are all compatible. The school also has an extensive range of software.

Mr Ives said computers attracted dirt and the old computer room had been dismal, but the new surroundings were encouraging the pupils to keep the suite looking attractive.

"The whole emphasis is on information technology for everyone and the idea is that it supports the pupils' normal school work and is not in addition to traditional subjects," he said.

Reproduced courtesy of the Newark Advertiser. *26 July 1991.*

Fashion boosts US trip

Pupils at Tuxford Comprehensive School show off some of the hats and clothes featured in a fashion show at the school on Tuesday.

They are (left to right) Katie Wetton (17), Deborah Daniels (16), Kirsty Rippard (15), Diana Quibell (16) and Claire Lyus (15).

Other models were teachers Mrs Judy Wright and Mrs Christine Carr, who organised the event, and parents Mrs Janet Medley and Mrs Sylvia Quibell.

The clothes were from Pause One Boutique of North Hykeham, which is run by Mrs Pauline Squire whose two sons attend the Tuxford school. The hats were from All Occasions, of Lincoln, which also has a shop in Collingham run by Mrs Joy Sanders.

The event raised £75 which will be used to help pay for an exchange visit to Dallas, USA, in May.

Reproduced courtesy of the *Newark Advertiser*. 29 April 1988.

School News 1

PALACE TO THE RESCUE!

Keith Atkinson, Headteacher of Tuxford School, a rural comprehensive in North Nottinghamshire, promised a new team strip to any soccer side who could bring back the County Cup for their age group. Tuxford, well known for its music, dance, drama and sport had never achieved such a feat since its opening in 1958.

As a weary, but jubilant, under sixteen side left the pitch, having thrashed Holgate School 6 - 0 in the final, they announced, "We want the Brazil shirts, Sir!".

True to his word Keith drove off into Nottingham, cheque book in hand, only to find, to his horror, that there were none available and that it was very unlikely that any would be available until March.

Since Tuxford now represent Nottinghamshire in the National Competition, the situation was desperate.

"Fortunately", explained successful soccer coach and Head of PE, Graham Curry, "I was watching Liverpool against Crystal Palace and noticed that the Palace away strip was the stylish yellow and green kit that we were looking for. I rang Palace and they couldn't have been more helpful. Realising we are a State Comprehensive School, rather than selling direct fom the Club Shop, they put us in touch with their suppliers in Scotland. Again, they too were tremendous. The shirts arrived within a week and we are ready to take on Leicestershire in the New Year - thanks to Palace.

Press release. January 1995.

Reflections on Mr Atkinson as Manager
The verdict of two independent consultants

Discussion with the staff of Tuxford Comprehensive School suggested that there is widespread agreement amongst them that it is a happy, purposeful institution and that its prevailing ethos and sense of achievement owe much to the personality and management style of the Head Teacher.

Although there was a clearly understood and shared overall aim to achieve academic respectability expressed through good examination results following comprehensivisation, the staff are currently unable to articulate the school's goals in any precise or detailed form. There is, nevertheless, a broad consensus that there exists a clear commitment to the pursuit of success, happiness and getting the best out of pupils and staff alike. A strong emphasis is placed upon the quality of relationships in a school which endeavours to provide each child 'with the maximum educational experience possible'. Everything undertaken is judged in terms of 'the benefit of the kids', and Tuxford overtly strives to be seen as not just a school but 'more a way of life'. All of this is consistently and powerfully reinforced by the Head Teacher's statements, style and actions, although there is no clear uniform perception shared by all staff.

Mr Atkinson has been described as presenting a somewhat Cavalier image. Lively, spontaneous, relaxed, flexible, highly approachable, witty and even irreverent, his enthusiasm and optimism are infectious and motivating. Believing in informality and personal mobility, he avoids his desk, lengthy formal meetings and documentation wherever it is possible and appropriate to do so. He enjoys great professional credibility in the eyes of the staff with whom he clearly aligns himself, always leads by example ('He would never ask anyone to do anything that he is not prepared to do himself'), and being a convinced exponent of the art of 'management by walking about', presents a strong and pervasive presence around the school which is perceived as being supportive rather than 'hovering' or interfering. He is fully involved in the school's considerable extra-curricular life – dramatic, musical, sporting and social – on which he places such high value.

Mr Atkinson, who has established cordial and productive relationships with his staff, believes in adopting a positive and liberal approach to management which stresses people's strengths, promotes and supports individual initiative, and devolves decision-making to senior managers and into the departments. He encourages and facilitates rather than directs change, giving colleagues a relatively free rein within the context of the school's over-arching philosophy and aims. ('There is never any limit set'.) He generates a feeling that everyone has a valid contribution to make and can be trusted to exercise sound professional judgement. He readily accepts and invites ideas from all levels within the school, his approach being inclusive and designed to enhance the individual's confidence and sense of self-worth.

Believing in co-operation, collaboration and peer-group pressure, he avoids personal confrontation and conflict wherever possible, seeing these as essentially destructive and counter-productive.

He is an excellent and accomplished public relations man who has done much to establish and promote the school's reputation and good standing in the local community. Adopting a slightly 'possessive' stance, he projects strong and, for parents, reassuring pride in Tuxford and its considerable achievements.

Mr Atkinson is therefore, a most effective and popular Head Teacher whose qualities are much appreciated by the school community that he leads.

It is within this context that the following issues are raised to provide a possible framework for reflection on practice.

1. Much of the discussion between staff is characterised by informality and rapid wit. There are, however, some staff who find it difficult to match, and therefore engage with, this style. There is a danger that these staff are unable to contribute as fully as they might wish and may even feel to some degree intimidated or excluded by it. Is this a real issue?

2. The Head Teacher's willingness to seek informal views on an issue from throughout the staff is welcomed by staff. How representative a view does this give? How random or selective is it? - partly because it will be linked with staff availability and partly because it offers enhanced influence to those most at ease with the style outlined in 1.

3. The vision of the Head Teacher appears to centre for staff and pupils on options of commitment, success, open opportunities, relationships. The coherence appears to stem from these over-arching notions rather than from detailed plans of pupil experience. Most staff find this engaging and motivating but some (new appointees, those who operate from a different framework) can feel disoriented or overwhelmed by the lack of detailed expectation. Is it possible/desirable to more fully/uniformly/formally communicate/debate the vision and its implications? Would such a communication help those who feel unsure and/or undermine the spontaneity of those who thrive on the freedom?

4. The good relationships in the school form a crucial enabling factor for development (the more so where an informal management style requires staff to trust each other and to be tolerant of, for example, overlap). What price is paid for the maintenance of good relationships? Are there some issues which are left damagingly to simmer and others which are passed to colleagues to manage any confrontation?

5. 1-4 make clear the strong staff support for much of the Head Teacher's management style. Should it, however, more obviously include other 'modes' so that, for example, formality, confrontation were seen to be employed as part of a repertoire on appropriate occasions? Would this undermine the over-riding management style?

School Log Book

1994-95

5 Sept. 94 - Staff Training Day. 6th Form signing on – 60 returned. Start of environmental improvements took place over the holiday including re-laying of drains at front of school. Seven new staff. Chairman of Governors, Mr Kitchen in to congratulate staff over exam performance.

6 Sept. 94 - (Y11) Pupils return. Nearly 950 on role. Induction day for 'A' level and GNVQ students. Lunches very late in Upper School.

9 Sept. 94 - Pressure of numbers evident – clear need for more car parking and classroom space.

14 Sept. 94 - School photograph day. School numbers continue to climb. Very wet day. Stress on basic infrastructure, walkways, corridors, etc.

18 Sept. 94 - Tuxford Ten road race. Soccer match on field. 'Crucible' rehearsal. Year 7 drains blocked.

19 Sept. 94 - 'Understanding industry' for GNVQ students. Chairman of Governors in to discuss progress of school management review. Curriculum Team meeting in evening.

28 Sept. 94 - Performance of the 'Crucible' - produced by Jenny Whittaker.

6 Oct. 94 - Margaret Fowkes – Special Needs AIS spent morning in school. Family of schools meeting in afternoon. Long listing of Director of Studies (applicants) by SMT.

11 Oct. 94 - Fire practice. Shortlist of Director of Studies applicants.

14 Oct. 94 - Yr 11 pupils to Retford for careers convention.

15 Oct. 94 - School Walk into Derbyshire – fine, bright day.

21 Oct. 94 - Inset closure day – Positive approaches to discipline. Trip to Berlin and Prague. School closes for half term.

106

2 Nov. 94 - Year 7 Tutor Evening – very good turn out.

9 Nov. 94 - Charity Fair.

10 Nov. 94 - Geography field trip to Whitby.

18 Nov. 94 - Disco Friday evening – good turn out – well behaved – similar event at Youth Wing.

24 Nov. 94 - Yr 11 pupils to Careers Conference in Nottingham.

24 Nov. 94 - Yr 11 exam week. Sixth form trip to 'Hot Stuff' – Theatre Royal Nottingham.

10 Dec. 94 - U16 side won the County Cup beating Holgate in the final 6 – 0. The first win for Tuxford School ever and the first in the Retford area since 1974.

14 Dec. 94 - Christmas lunch.

16 Dec. 94 - School closed early. Ski trip off to Austria.

SPRING TERM 1995

9 Jan. 95 - Year 13 Mock examinations. Jo Baker in to promote D of E and Youth service. Governors F and GP meeting in evening – Mr Longden outlined the 1995/96 Budget – cuts involved.

12 Jan. 95 - Budget meeting in Retford – 4% cuts predicted.

16 Jan. 95 - Training day on assessment.

18 Jan. 95 - Year 11 field trip to Lincoln. School cross country championships. Reception at Retford Town Hall for soccer team. Senior Management Team meeting – wide ranging agenda.

25 Jan. 95 - North Notts Cross Country Championships – Tuxford overall winners and junior girls. Yr11 parents evening – very good and positive turn out.

27 Jan. 95 - Snowy afternoon – school closure. D of E Presentation in Youth Wing disrupted.

10 Feb. 95 - Non-Uniform Day. Disco in evening.

28 Feb. 95 - Retford/Tuxford Heads discussion on rationalisation of GNVQ courses – particularly in the light of budget cuts. John Culpin in all day – department planning review.

107

8 Mar. 95 - Auditors in school. Year 9 parents evening held in lower school due to drama practice of 'Mysteries' in main hall.

9 Mar. 95 - Carol Lowe (Governor) in to discuss library appeal in an attempt to increase book stock from 3 to 5 per child.

13 Mar. 95 - Staff meeting – effect of budget cuts. Meeting at Edwinstowe to clear brief for Bassetlaw. Higher Education conference at Birmingham.
F & GP meeting in evening – redundancy discussed – approval in principle to be seen by full Governors next week.

15 Mar. 95 - Staff Training Day – coursework and exam preparation

17 Mar. 95 - Yr 8 Science Museum visit organised by Liz Briggs. Tony Hyman – Youth & Community – possible extension to Youth Wing activities. Comic relief Day.

20 Mar. 95 - Governors full meeting to discuss budget. Approved with no loss of staff.
Tuxford School Association – arrange reunion.

25 Mar. 95 - HM and Janet Poorta attend 'Fight Against Cuts in Education' rally in London.

27 Mar. 95 - 'Mysteries' begins a week's run.

30 Mar. 95 - Fred Riddell – Chairman of Education Committee to see Mysteries – he felt that it was one of the best productions he had seen over the past ten years – he congratulated John Perry Head of Drama.

5 Apr. 95 - HM ill.

7 Apr. 95 - Yrs 11, 12 and 13 stood down. Barnardos Easter Extravaganza at Palace Theatre fronted by Mrs Jenny Whittaker – dance and music content from the school, family and friends of the school. School closes for Easter.

SUMMER TERM 1995

24 Apr. 95 - School opens. Wet, cold day. Heating in lower school down!

29 Apr. 95 (Saturday) - Eden Camp visit. John Gibson and Yr 9 pupils

1 May 95 - Training Day Closure – OFSTED issues. R Hyde (AIS) spoke to all staff re above.

3 May 95 (Wednesday) - Yr 10 Parents Evening

4 May 95 - *Governors Health and Safety Check. Oxfam Workshop all day – reps from Oxfam working with Year 8 pupils. Funeral of B Woodward (previous headteacher). Dick Fursey and HM attended on behalf of staff.*

8 May 95 - *School Closure VE Day.*

9 May 95 - *Dawn Benzies school IIP consultant to review Investor in People evidence with Joyce Hallam and Dick Fursey. SAT's exams for Yr 9. History Field Visits by Yr 10 students to Lincoln with John Gibson, Steve Smith and Ann Evans*

10 May 95 - *Yr8 girls won North Notts Athletics. History Field Visits by Yr 10 students to Lincoln with John Gibson, Steve Smith and Ann Evans*

11 May 95 (Saturday) - *Tuxford students reunion in hall. Pupils involved – 15 mile Oxfam sponsored Walk.*

20 May 95 - *KA absent all week. GCSE exams start today plus exam week for all Year 7-10 pupils. Full Governing body meeting.*

21 May 95 - *Young Enterprise presentations for Bassetlaw Schools at Retford Town Hall. The school business group won three awards (best ever!!) and Louise Douglas gave a vote of thanks to all present as she was voted Achiever of the Year.*

27 May 95 - *Dick Fursey attended BASH (Bassetlaw Secondary Heads) meeting – great concern expressed by Heads over possible continuing budget cuts next year.*

5 Jun. 95 - *J Regan in school (Investors in People) pre assessor to study storyboard and portfolio of evidence.*

Investors in People.

On Task, On Target *The story of the first fifty years of Tuxford School*

Chris Knott.

7 Jun. 95 - GNVQ verifier in school all day. Full Governors meeting 6.30 – job description and advert for Deputy Headship approved.

12 Jun. 95 - HM absent all week. School timings adjusted to ease passage of pm. GCSE and A Level exams – 3 period morning and 3 period afternoon.

13 Jun. 95 - Half time post for Modern Languages to be advertised.

16 Jun. 95 - Advert for Deputy Headship published in TES. Many requests for further information.

20 Jun. 95 - Decision taken to advertise internally for assistant heads of year posts – no money available for post holders at present.

21 Jun. 95 - Wacky Walk took place pm. Final venue Sutton on Trent Primary School. Absolute secrecy was maintained - glorious weather. Outstanding feature was the games on arrival organised by Scott Colton and younger members of staff.

Mr Atkinson hands out the awards at Tuxfor's sports day.

22 Jun. 95 - Chris Knott and 2 upper school pupils visited the 'Young Engineers for Britain' conference at Nottingham. All Yr 12 Geography students visited Nottingham also - A Level field work.

26 Jun. 95 - Yr 10 Sports Day – weather fine.

27 Jun. 95 - HM returned to school. 'Moving On' briefing meeting held in school – Roger May in chair and over 20 businesses represented. Yr 10 to Higher Education Fayre.

28 Jun. 95 - New Intake Day – pupils in afternoon, parents and pupils in evening. Meeting of Consortium Budget Managers in school re Ground Maintenance.

29 Jun. 95 - Yr 7 and 8 Sports Day am – glorious weather. Many school records *broken. Governors in school to shortlist for Deputy Head post.*

30 Jun. 95 - *Dave Cotton and 30 Yr 10 pupils on trip to American Adventure (Park) all day on Maths assignments!! Closing date for Modern Languages Post – most applicants cannot start until January 1st.*

6 Jul. 95 - *Mervyn Griffiths – OFSTED RGI – in to meet HM, Beth Soule and Tina Powell re inspection in October. Furniture delivered to new room.*

7 Jul. 95 - *'Moving on' Conference sponsored by NNTEC. All Year 10 involved – very good event organised by Roger May. Dick Jenkinson in to discuss survey of Leisure and Learning needs in Tuxford area.*

Dave Cotton.

10 Jul. 95 - *Work experience underway. Interviews for Deputy Head to replace Mr R Fursey. Mrs E Soule appointed. Curriculum Committee discuss OFSTED issues.*

12 Jul. 95 - *Ukrainian party arrives – exchange visit with staff and pupils. Senior Management meet.*

13 Jul. 95 - *Y12 camp returns. Mrs Soule and Mrs Powell went through Governors OFSTED inspection responsibilities. Annual Parents meeting – lively debate about funding and GMS. Action group set up.*

Dick Fursey.

15 Jul. 95 (Saturday) - *Dick Fursey retirement party at Ann Allwood's.*

17 Jul. 95 - *Activities Week – camps out. Work experience continues. Ukrainian visitors on site.*

18 Jul. 95 - *Evening Post on site to look at PE facilities (or lack of them).*

20 Jul. 95 - *Jim Kitchen (Chair of Governors) in to see HM over future plans. Afternoon meeting on the development of a Sports Centre at Tuxford.*

25 Jul. 95 - *School closes for Summer vacation.*

Tina Powell.

111

Mr Atkinson's School

Keith Atkinson was usually addressed as "Boss" by his staff. Some would call him by his first name and others might sometimes refer to him as "Acko" but they all had a very real respect for him. As headteacher he was a showman, a larger than life personality who cared passionately about the school and who lost no opportunity to tell others of his enthusiasm. As a head and as a person he was positive, vigorous, outspoken and encouraging.

He was headteacher of Tuxford School from September 1978 to the end of February 1996 when he was forced to take early retirement to battle with multiple sclerosis. During his seventeen and a half years in office he raised the aspirations and achievements of the school significantly. At the start of his headship some parents living in the official catchment area chose to send their children to former grammar schools in nearby towns; by the end of his time at the helm thirty percent of the school's intake lived outside the catchment area. The school's sixth form started with just 11 students in 1980 and by 1996 it had 148. The staying on rate rose from thirty percent in 1984 to over fifty percent before he retired. Another achievement was that Mr Atkinson also maintained the school's focus during implementation of major changes to management, curriculum and assessment imposed by national education reforms. Below are some of the key events of his years as headteacher:

1980   Sixth form opened – just 11 students from last secondary modern intake.
        Two word processors purchased for the school

1982   Corporal punishment phased out in county schools during 1982/83 following a decision of the European Court of Human Rights – ahead of legislation in 1986 abolishing it throughout the country from September 1987. Poor public examination results seen as a turning point in the school's history.

1985   Bitter teachers' pay dispute disrupted extra-curricular activities

1986   GCSE syllabuses were introduced in September (to be examined for the first time in May/June 1988). Education Act reorganised Governing Bodies to give parents a greater influence.

1987   County dropped proposal to scrap school sixth forms

1988   Education Reform Act introduced the national curriculum (phased in before 1992) and local management of schools (from 1990). Decision to simplify school name by dropping "Comprehensive". School houses discontinued.

1991   Rooms re-allocated to create department "suites" – except for Year 7 teaching rooms.

1992   Farm unit phased out

1995   First Ofsted inspection of Tuxford School in October

For its first four years under the leadership of Mr Atkinson the school was still adjusting to being a comprehensive and he was making his presence felt about the school whilst taking stock of existing policies and of his new colleagues. At the end of this period of adjustment, in 1982, fifth year students produced the worst set of exam results that the school had known before - or since. The uphill path set for his predecessor, Bernard Woodward, in 1976 (to return to an earlier visualisation) had brought the new head to the edge of marshland. Through force of personality he led everyone across and after that he set a cracking pace, through pleasant fields once more, towards the triumphant first Ofsted inspection and a Good School Award.

The faculty system imposed by county in 1976 had been a public relations disaster. Not only had subject staff been lumped together in unequal, unwieldy and unmanageable groups, but also long-established heads of department felt demotivated and under-valued. Dennis Knox, the deputy headteacher responsible for the curriculum, and the four Faculty Directors (Warren Cookson for Maths, Science and Business Studies; Chris Knott for Creative Design and Technology; Richard Martin for Environmental, Community and Recreational Studies and Peter Rickerby for Humanities and Languages) met as a curriculum committee and they were able to push through useful changes, but decision-making was very much "top down" rather than enthusiastic participation. Mr Atkinson soon realised that this had to change, so as the Directors moved on to new roles the faculties were quietly disbanded and the authority of heads of department was restored. Peter Rickerby left in December 1980 and Warren Cookson became head of sixth form in 1984. Mr Knox gave up his

Mr Atkinson set the pace for Tuxford school.

oversight of curriculum in 1983 (when George Jeffcott retired) to focus on administration so this also contributed to disbanding the faculty system.

The last few secondary modern intakes produced pleasing results. Mr Atkinson proudly reported the 1979 and 1980 results in both GCE and CSE to governors. He told them that the first comprehensive intake had done well too: "A record number of CSE and 'O' level exams were taken this term and the results were very good indeed – 25 pupils gaining 5 'O' levels or more." (1) However in the following year the numbers achieving this level of success plummeted and Mr Atkinson wrote: "Results were mixed and tended to be influenced by a reduction in dual entries where candidates take both 'O' level and CSE in the same subject and pay the entry fee for one of them." (2)

Former Physics teacher Roger Longden remembered the situation well: "Keith realised that he had to shake the place up. The turning point came when we had disappointing GCE results from a full ability range (comprehensive) intake – in 1982 I think. On the first day of the next academic year Keith gave us his stark assessment. In the meeting room of the "Lower School" (later the library in the Clumber Building) he told the assembled staff, 'These results are crap. You now have a choice: if you continue to produce results of this calibre the best students will drift away from Tuxford, in increasing numbers, this place will close and you lot will be out of a job, but if we get cracking, show that we can deliver the

113

Back Row: Debra Hinds, Maggie Aiston, Terry White, Richard Martin, John Parker, Stuart Smith, Phil Baker, Roger Longden, Graham Curry, Oliver Foreman, Bill Roe, Dick Fursey, Peter Baxter, Jeff Brookes, Chris Knott, John Perry, Keith Atkinson, Mick Keeling, Dave Cook, Ian Chappell, Pete Searle, John Parfrement, Roger May, Gris Stevens.
Front row: Nicki Shaw, Nurse Brecke, Val Slack, Carol Westbury, Jenny Whittaker, Jo Chapman, Heather Foster, Beth Soule, name unknown, Barbara Burton, Mavis Paling, Christine Carr, Carole Wall, Cathie Town, Eileen Fleetwood, Tina Powell, Janet Poorta, Yvonne Guy, Rhona Ward, Tony Lynch, Julie Hethershaw,

results whilst keeping our reputation as a quiet well-ordered school we will clean up.' His logic was that as a secondary modern turned comprehensive our standards would be seen to rise whereas in grammar schools turned comprehensive standards would be seen to fall.

"Keith always gave the impression that he was ad libbing and talking spontaneously from conviction, but I later came to know that every word would have been carefully rehearsed. The impact of the talk was dramatic. By now there were several keen recently-appointed staff in most subject areas and they went away resolved to rise to the challenge. The talk was more remarkable because it was given at a time, before league tables, when there was very little mention of results in the press, etc.

"Needless to say, Keith's strategy, first articulated at that historic pivotal moment in 1982, worked. The results went up and students were keen to come here from Ollerton, Retford and Newark and the places between. That staff briefing in 1982 was the turning point for Tuxford School." (3)

Dennis Knox offered me an insight into another aspect of Mr Atkinson's strategy for improvement: "Most of the students were village children and their parents did not have high expectations of education. Many of the village schools did a good job in preparing the children, but the parents didn't seem too bothered. When Mr Atkinson came he changed perceptions. He was particularly good at public relations. He talked to parents and led them to expect more. He also used public relations in the staffroom and he got everyone to work together. He had a wonderful way of putting a message across without looking as though he was putting it across." (4)

The real secret of Mr Atkinson's success, according to Geoff Lloyd who is currently deputy headteacher of the school in 2007, is that he built the staff into a team that felt both strong and determined to prove a point: "Being so far from the centres of power and influence over the years we have developed a Tuxford fighting spirit. We say, 'This is our deck of cards, we don't like it, but we will play it well. The buildings may not be as good as they've got down the road, but we will still go on and be successful.' That was Keith's attitude. He got annoyed if our efforts were minimised - and I think that's what pulls us together. We are determined to show them: 'We'll do it in spite of you, we'll do it with these crap facilities. We'll get 33 kids doing A Level Chemistry! We won't use this as an excuse for failure, we'll use it as a springboard for success.' I think that has permeated through staff and I hope that continues into the new school." (5)

Elsie Pickering watching students playing chess.

When he took up his post Mr Atkinson estimated that possibly forty bright students from the catchment area had gone elsewhere for their education – some to grammar schools in Retford which were reorganised after Tuxford. This initial loss of talented students from the north of the catchment area would have had an impact on early results. In 1984 there were still some parents who needed convincing that a former secondary modern could be a good choice: "Several Elkesley parents are anxious about their children coming to Tuxford. I invite anyone who has worries about a transfer to visit the school and make up their own minds about it." (6) By 1992 the shortfall in intake was just a memory: "It is a measure of the spectacular success of a hard working and highly professional staff that this situation has been completely reversed – not only that but exam results comfortably outperform all the old Grammar Schools." (7)

All the evidence suggests that Tuxford School had been an orderly and well-disciplined place before 1973 because deputy headteacher George Jeffcott had ensured that standards of behaviour were high when the school had been a comparatively small and compact secondary modern. (Nevertheless, at least two teachers who experienced discipline problems in their lessons have been identified by people who contributed to my research – and the behaviour of Tuxford students sent to Newark Technical College for "link courses" was often worse than in school). We have noted already that when numbers on roll expanded rapidly following the raising of the school leaving age the system of supervision proved somewhat inadequate. The campus area had expanded with the opening of two new teaching blocks so one person could no longer supervise everywhere and some older children – often the ones who were reluctant learners – needed to be kept occupied. Heads of Year under the leadership of deputy head Elsie Pickering took on an increasingly important role for "pastoral care." At the same time Mr Atkinson was not prepared to compromise on standards. He soon established a zero tolerance policy and enforced it rigorously - even after corporal punishment was no longer permitted in 1982. We have already noted a student reaction to the new head expressed by Carol Brumpton, a member of the third year when he arrived: "When Mr Atkinson…

arrived, I was scared to death of him. Even though Mr Jeffcott was scary he was much more so." (8)

In September 1984 the headteacher told governors: "Few exclusions took place this (summer) term but swearing has joined smoking, fighting and disrespect to staff as grounds for exclusion. The reason for this was that staff generally felt that standards of language had slipped…" (9) Geoff Lloyd recalled that: "…Keith always did duty at break and on the dinner queue. He was quite forceful with (the students). That was quite useful. He would exclude quite quickly and rightly so, and when you excluded then it hurt… He had a zero tolerance policy towards smoking and swearing: if caught they were instantly out. Parents felt this was a quality of the school and it helped to make the school popular." (5)

A number of reasons for the school's good behaviour record have been suggested down the years. Perhaps it is because the children live in the countryside instead of in towns. Perhaps it is because school policies and rule enforcement are effective. Perhaps it is because the place has always had a happy atmosphere and a good sense of humour. Certainly Mr Atkinson encouraged his staff to be active and to provide students with opportunities and experiences to make them appreciate their education: "Not so much a school, more a way of life." In February 1980 he led the first ski-ing trip to Vetrilo in northern Italy. Teachers Mick Keeling, Bill Roe and Luann Roper helped him to supervise the twenty nine students. Tuxford Topics, the school newsletter started in 1978, offers a reasonably complete record of school life from September 1984. The edition of that month offers an interesting insight into extra-curricular life in school: "Best sports season ever: 6 Soccer finals – winning 2; 4 Cricket finals – U15 beat Lilley & Stone, Grove and Magnus in the final. Sellout concerts: 'Oliver' and 'Cats' – rave reviews – practice begins for 'Fiddler on the Roof'. Foreign visits: France, Italy, Texas, Monaco – exchanges planned with Grenoble and Dallas! Summer School (in holiday): 400 attended to water-ski, wind-surf, row, scull, roller disco… Camps: Norfolk, Snowdonia, Derbyshire, Lake District." (9)

Mr Atkinson was particularly keen to promote

Reproduced courtesy of *The Independent*. 31 Dec 1992.

Independent 31 Dec 1992

Talent: (back row, left to right) Melanie Burman, Shelley Whetton, William Hill, James Valentine; (front, left to right) Richard Alvey, Edward Martin, Clare Price, Adam Schofield   Photograph: Claire Mackintosh/Empics

Please Sir, pump up the volume

When Tuxford School's band steps out of the recording studio to do a gig, the headteacher comes along as roadie. **Julia Hagedorn reports** sport and musical or drama productions on stage – and a brief look at his main interest out of school will help to explain why. He had been Captain of Boats at Durham University in his student days and he was captain of Nottingham Boat Club from 1961 to 1974. The year before he came to Tuxford he was elected its president (and at the time of writing in 2007 he is still the president of the club). After the opening of Holme Pierrepoint National Water Sports Centre he was involved at the top level in organising, managing and officiating major rowing events on a regular basis including the national championships. He helped to organise the world junior rowing championship in 1973 and the world rowing championships of 1975 and 1986. For the latter he was responsible for accommodation and dining arrangements for 1500 athletes. Clearly he was actively involved in sport. As for the music, the Boat Club building beside the Trent and Nottingham Forest's football ground became an important if intimate venue for live music in the 1960s and 70s whilst he was club captain. It could only hold an audience of 300 but it hosted such stars as Alexis Korner, Brian Auger, Chris Farlow, John Mayall, Zoot Money, Geno Washington, Def Leppard, Rod Stewart, Led Zeppelin, Jethro Tull and Eric Clapton. In the 90's the school rock group created by head of music Ian Chappell, was invited to play at the Boat Club on several occasions.

In 1982 Mr Atkinson organised the first "Tuxford 10" for the local community, a ten mile circular road race from Tuxford through Egmanton, Normanton-on-Trent and Skegby in aid of asthma research. Typically competitive and confident, he challenged everyone taking part to try to beat him by promising a £1 donation to charity for everyone who crossed the finishing line before him. Forty people accepted the challenge, many a lot younger than him, but he did not have to pay much because he finished fifth. History teacher Freddie White led a group of sixth formers to start the race, to provide refreshments around the course and to record the results. Certificates and medals were made by art teacher Peter Searle and craft teacher Chris Knott respectively. After the race Mr Atkinson promised to make the event bigger and better in the following year. "I aim to put over 250 competitors on to the road next year and I'm looking for local sponsorship," he told the Retford Times. (10)

Mr Atkinson led the school by setting an example of dedication and energy. He was a keen member of the team organising school discos – and they became very professional with an impressive light show and "smoke" generator. For the staff, Mr Atkinson's "can do" approach was infectious.

Geoff Lloyd remembers how the staff rolled up their sleeves and got on with improving science facilities in the late 80s: "The early days were really exciting because it was going forward. We partitioned the back of the science lab and built a prep room. That was really good. Later we re-did Science 1 and Science 2. We converted the rural studies room, then we converted the old needlework room. I don't think I had very much to do with the money at that stage for those things. There was money from High Marnham and the LEA contributed… Roger and I were decorating Heather's room when it was actually an NASUWT strike day. We finished

Pictured here are some of the runners in the annual Tuxford Ten. It attracted runners from all over the area. Sept 1987.

painting it and then Dennis came in and threw us off-site. He let us know that we were not insured to be on site. But that's the sort of thing we did. That was a good laugh." (5)

Several areas of the school buildings were improved by staff initiative. Dave Ives, formerly of the Maths department but by then head of ICT, wired up the school's first computer room in RoSLA, for example. A cable network was later established throughout the school by him. In 1988 the main library was moved into the lower school building and its former base at the back of the quadrangle became the drama studio. Carole Wall and John Perry had to work very hard to achieve the move during a school holiday. Similarly, in 1993 the sixth form took over the science laboratory in lower school as a study area so Mick Keeling and Dave Cook made the necessary modifications.

Food technology teacher Julie Hethershaw remembered one of the school's fund-raising events: "One of the best fun events that I helped with was the series of Wacky Walks. These began when the school needed to raise money for a minibus – at about the time when the teachers' national work-to-rule dispute ended in 1986. Only two or three weeks' preparation time was available for the first Wacky Walk… so Oliver (Foreman) said he would concentrate on arranging the walk if I would organise the barbecue… Unfortunately the whole event turned into a potential disaster for me as every break time Oliver would revise the number upwards when more and more forms were handed in. On the morning of the event I got to school really early and the Head, Keith Atkinson, saw me looking agitated and he asked why I was pacing up and down... However, I needn't have worried. The weather was the best possible and the participants' arrival at the barbecue was spaced by their walking ability… Everyone had a burger and a drink so I was relieved and we all enjoyed the event so much that we repeated it a few times. The 'wacky' feature of the first walk is that staff dressed as characters from the Tales of Robin Hood. Some of the men hid up trees and the pupils had the task of spotting them. Another feature of the event was that the location was kept secret so parents had to phone school to find where they needed to go to collect their offspring. A lovely party atmosphere was created for all." (11)

Miss Hethershaw also told me how the female staff of the school started to organise a dining club: "One aspect of Tuxford life that has been great fun for me is the 'Gossip Club'. It started in the 1980's when Maggie Aiston, Carol Westbury, Ann Napier and I got together out of school for a chat and a shared meal. Maggie made the most magnificent puddings! We usually met at my house. After a while one or two female colleagues started coming along and then one or two more. A casual remark by John Parker (science teacher) provided the name for our group that has stuck. At our most recent meeting, in a restaurant in Worksop, there were 22 of us – which I feel is too many. We enjoy discussing wines, films etc rather than actually gossiping!"

Anecdotes of the Atkinson years often include John Parker. Science and ICT teacher Tony Lynch remembered his skills in the classroom: "John's great strength was in knowing how to teach students by tapping into their everyday experiences. He drew fantastic cartoons in lessons, all in an effort

Early school computers.

to get a point across. He is the only person I have ever seen who, during a lesson, could transform a sketch of the female reproductive system into one of the FA cup. Have a look at a Biology text book and you might see what he meant. Boys only interested in football were suddenly gaining high marks in Biology - all down to JP.

"I still meet ex-pupils who remember when John gave them a pet rock to look after, complete with a small bag of gravel as food. He told them that their new pet might not move very much, but that with care, over time it would absorb the gravel and grow, albeit very slowly. It worries me at times to think that there is someone out there carefully tending a piece of limestone in the hope that one day it might move just a little bit.

Carol Westbury.

"He once asked me to bring a completely new set of clothes to work, and to get changed during break time. He had been doing a series of lessons about inheritance, and somehow had convinced his students that I had an identical twin called Billy. According to John, Billy came to school quite often to give me a break from my lessons. I duly appeared after morning break, dressed completely differently, and trying to act in an unusual manner. John greeted me with a "Hello Billy!", and a class full of students watched me in complete silence as I walked though their classroom. In the staff room at break, he cried with laughter, but told me that every single pupil understood the point he was making." (12)

Cathie Town shared memories of another teacher, but John Parker was included in her story too: "Christine Carr was known as "The Duchess" and the nice thing was that she knew it and was able to laugh at herself. Her image was twinset & pearls and she was very much the 'Lady'. She would expect nothing less than men opening doors for her - and would stand and wait until they did so. She taught what was known as 'Office Practice', and then went on to teach English. Chris was always involved with the school trips and would always expect people to carry her suitcase. She was not very punctual so everyone learned to tell her to be wherever she was meeting them a good half hour prior to the actual time needed for any events as this was the only way to ensure she would make it for the right time.

"On one very memorable day Chris was very distraught, as she had managed to get a stain on her skirt. It was suggested that she should go the science department where they would probably have something to get rid of it. Chris innocently asked John Parker for his help. He told her that he'd try but she would have to take her skirt off and take refuge in the dark room while he dealt with the problem. JP, being JP, didn't get the skirt back to her for about an hour after. Chris was not very pleased but everyone else enjoyed the story.

"One school trip was to Berlin, and Mr Marshall (coach driver) had his passport stolen. Chris Carr and Mick Keeling went with him to the British Consulate and he was getting nowhere until Chris Carr, with her beautiful manicured nails, tapped repeatedly on the desk and said, 'Now look here young man, I know the Sheriff of Nottingham, and if this mess is not sorted out now, I will telephone every national newspaper to tell them that a coach full of British students is stuck in Berlin because you are not doing your job properly.'" (13)

Dennis Knox is another person remembered in school folklore. Former art teacher Peter

119

Searle told me this story about him: "(Dennis Knox) seemed to upset both John Parfrement (then woodwork teacher) and myself in the same afternoon. Knowing he was teaching last lesson that day we determined to get our own back! His office was to the right of the main entrance steps with a double window. We emptied his office of all furniture onto the grass outside. Desk, chair, filing cabinet etc. Just as we closed the window and put his phone on the desk, it rang. At that moment Mr Atkinson, the Headmaster, came up the steps with two parents. I answered the phone and informed Mr Atkinson that is was the Area Education Office for him. He asked me to inform them that he was busy and would call back. He walked off with the parents and never made any mention of the re-location of the office. Neither did Dennis. Neither did he upset us again. Neither did we return his furniture!!" (14)

Geoff Lloyd told me about another deputy headteacher: "Elsie (Pickering) was pastoral deputy and girls' welfare - and it was always my register that went missing so I was always in trouble with Elsie, I used to do my register and then go into teaching and even now when I see Elsie she says I've got to stop it because she's sending my register off. I got to know Elsie more than I got to see Bob (Taylor, another deputy head). I would have said she was the one who kept Keith in check. He would often start a conversation and then walk away from you because he was needed somewhere else - as Heads do. I can remember Elsie saying, 'Come back here Keith, don't walk away from me.' She was quite a powerful lady and again right for the school at that time. Elsie was very open, you could talk to Elsie about anything, she used to say, 'Now my dear…' to you." (5)

Farewell dinner for deputy head

Retiring after 25 years at Tuxford Comprehensive School is deputy head, Mr. George Jeffcott (centre) pictured after a retirement dinner specially made by pupils Andrea Bracegirdle and Cheryl Davison.
Photo ref: B1803.

TUXFORD Comprehensive school's deputy headmaster George Jeffcott was served a special treat to mark his retirement.

For some of the pupils cooked up a farewell meal to honour his 25 years service at the school and he was also the special guest at a party and disco.

South Wales-born Mr. Jeffcott started teaching maths and physical education at the Tux-ford school in 1958 and has soon a flight-lieutenant, he joined a teacher training scheme and qualified for the Nottinghamshire education authority after 1½ years.

He started teaching at a New-ark school before moving to West Bridgford for seven years and then to Flintham where the headmaster was a former member of the Dambusters Squadron.

Following his retirement Mr. Jeffcott intends to spend time looking after the garden at his

Mr Atkinson was always being talked about too. When he decided that he no longer needed his own office there was some surprise. When he offered to pay a contribution towards a conservatory to expand the staffroom there was even more surprise. But no-one expected any less of him when they heard that he had ordered a rubber stamp bearing just eight capital letters so that annoying documents from county or the DfES could be filed under B for Bullshit.

A very different type of memory was shared by Dennis Knox. Long-serving deputy head George Jeffcott - who has been featured in these pages from the start of our story - retired in 1983. Unfortunately he did not enjoy the long and happy retirement that he deserved: "Not many years after his retirement Mr Jeffcott committed suicide. However, he was not depressed – and he was certainly not depressed at school. He often said in normal conversation that if ever he

Reproduced courtesy of the *Retford Times*. July 1983.

School bridging gap to employment

Reproduced courtesy of the *Retford Times*. 27 Oct 1995.

became seriously ill he would shoot himself. Everybody used to say, 'No you won't, don't be daft.' After he retired he got cancer, I think it was cancer of the lungs, and he came round to my house to see me one day and I hardly recognised him because he had lost so much weight. However, he was still the same Jeff in spirits and he was getting over the illness. It wasn't long after that that he thought he had a brain tumour – so he went out and shot himself. When they did

TUXFORD Comprehensive had two reasons to celebrate this month after opening a Partnership Room, and receiving an "Investor in People" award.

The new Partnership Room is a joint effort between the school and North Notts Training and Enterprise Council, and will mean that the school, along with local businesses and community groups, will now be able to use the room for a variety of activities.

Award

Headmaster at Tuxford Comprehensive Keith Atkinson said: "The room is excellent. A lot of work has gone into setting it up, both from staff at the school and at North Notts TEC.

"The room has a number of facilities which means it can be hired out for meetings, visual displays, and other group projects."

Chief Executive of North Notts TEC, Pat Richards is impressed and encouraged by the new project.

"We are keen to provide an opportunity for schools to open up their resources to the community. At the same time we are working towards bridging the gap between education and

● TUXFORD Comprehensive celebrate the opening of the schools new Partnership Room.

Pictured at the opening is Headmaster Keith Atkinson, Project Manager, Dick Fursey, Chief Executive of the TEC, Pat Richards, and Elizabeth Soel.

employment."

The day was also marked by the presentation of a plaque to acknowledge the school as an "Investor In People."

Judged by Dawn Benzies, an independent consultant, the school was assessed and found to meet the set criteria that enabled them to gain the award.

Dick Fursey who recently retired from teaching at the school was involved in the scheme from the beginning. He said: "The build-up throughout the whole of the scheme brought the staff involved closer together, it made us work as a close team."

Tuxford Comprehensive is the only school in

Bassetlaw to gain this kind of recognition and is one of a group of 150 schools in the whole of the country to receive it.

Keith Atkinson said: "There are around 25,000 schools in the country which means that to be one of only 150 schools in the UK to receive this award is some achievement."

the post mortem he didn't have a brain tumour at all." (4)

Mr Atkinson worked with seven deputies during his years as headteacher: George Jeffcott, Dennis Knox and Elsie Pickering; Trevis Woodward, who taught Maths, left to become an inspector in Lincolnshire and became a headteacher in Wales; Bob Taylor, an English teacher went on to become a headteacher after three years as a deputy; Dick Fursey, who had been appointed as co-ordinator of lower school when Tuxford went comprehensive; Beth Soule, drama teacher and head of English who was an energetic acting head for two terms after Mr Atkinson retired and is currently, in 2007, a headteacher in Suffolk.

Before Mr Atkinson retired he restructured the school's top management. In line with the custom in other schools the Policy Committee was renamed the Senior Management Team. Elsie Pickering retired in 1990 and then both Dennis Knox and Dick Fursey retired in 1995 so he was then able to reduce the number of deputies from three to one, but built a larger senior team around him. Geoff Lloyd became assistant headteacher responsible for the curriculum in 1994 and he remembered the last 18 months of Mr Atkinson's headship: "Keith was already ill at the time. There were certain things he could have managed quite easily five or six years before that became quite difficult for him to manage. He may have been less patient with staff situations than he had been previously but I think that desire to be successful had always been strong in him. We had to manage a holding operation, that was good fun for a bit and it wasn't really a problem. He had built in the capacity for that to happen. He had a good senior team around him…" (5)

Mick Keeling had taught at the school throughout the Atkinson era and he had expected The Boss to leave in style: "The manner of Keith Atkinson's leaving was sad. He didn't get the chance to choose his day. I didn't get the chance to shake his hand properly and say 'See you around Keith' because he just went. His leaving 'do' was not the same as it would have been if he had gone in high spirits with a happy retirement to contemplate. I felt at the time that with his departure the school lost momentum for a while." (15)

Mr Atkinson's arrival at his retirement party was suitably eye-catching. He was collected from his Southwell home by Sutton-on-Trent bus operator John Marshall in a vintage single decker bus. Stylish though this was, the headline-grabbing conclusion to his headship came at the beginning of 1997 when he was awarded the M.B.E. in the New Year's Honours for services to the school and to rowing. It was fitting that a man who always enjoyed the big occasion as headteacher and who was so competitive could bid farewell to the school in such ostentatious style.

Sources

1   *Headteacher's Report to Governing Body September 1981*, Keith Atkinson, Tuxford School Archive Papers, unpublished

2   *Headteacher's Report to Governing Body September 1982*, Keith Atkinson, Tuxford School Archive Papers, unpublished

3   *My early days at Tuxford, Roger Longden Tuxford School Archive Papers*, unpublished, 2006

4   *A View from Policy Committee*, Dennis Knox, Tuxford School Archive Papers, unpublished, 2007

5   *The Best Career Move I've Ever Made*, Geoff Lloyd, Tuxford School Archive Papers, unpublished, 2007

6   *Headteacher's Report to Governing Body May 1984*, Keith Atkinson, Tuxford School Archive Papers, unpublished

7   *Headteacher's Report to Governing Body September 1992*, Keith Atkinson, Tuxford School Archive Papers, unpublished

8   *Tuxford's first Comprehensive Intake*, Carol Brumpton, Tuxford School Archive Papers, unpublished, 2007

9   *Tuxford Topics September 1984*, Tuxford School publication, 1984

10   *Top Marks*, Retford Times, 8 October 1982

11   *My Career at Tuxford*, Julie Hethershaw, Tuxford School Archive Papers, unpublished, 2006

12   *Thoughts on John – Funeral oration*, Tony Lynch, Tuxford School Archive Papers, unpublished, 2005

13   *Sunlight and mini-skirts* by Cathie Town, Tuxford School Archive Papers, unpublished, 2005

14   *Tuxford School Anecdotes*, Peter Searle, Tuxford School Archive Papers, unpublished, 2005

15   *Thirty Two Years & Three Headteachers*, Mick Keeling, Tuxford School Archive Papers, unpublished, 2007

Bob Taylor.

Sir takes the disco blues rap

● DEPUTY headmaster Bob Taylor is bottom of the charts after flogging his school's entire collection of disco records.

● He thought he was a HIT when youngsters flocked to his stall at the school's spring fair and snapped up brand new records for just 10p a time.

● But he knew he was a MISS when fifth-formers at Tuxford Comprehensive School, near Retford, Notts, wanted the records for their disco.

● "It wasn't my fault. I don't know one disco record from another. I'm a classical man myself," said Bob, 36. Now he is raising money to buy a new collection.

Reproduced courtesy of the *Sun Newspaper*. 10 Apr 1987.

122

© TUXFORD 1988.

The Hunchback of Notre Dame.

1988 School Production

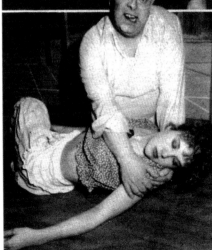

Staff make the models

MEMBERS of staff at Tuxford School had their faces encased in plaster last week.

The event was organised by Head of Art, Mr Peter Searle, as part of the preparations for the stage set of the school's latest musical production, The Hunchback of Notre Dame.

Music for the production has been composed by Head of Music, Mr Chappell, and the words by Head of Drama, Mr Perry.

Explained Mr Searle wanted some really gargoyles to set about entrance to the Cath staff were o

Keith Atkinson's thoughts on retirement, 1996
Responses to questions from Sixth Form students

I'm not totally happy with what's going on. As you know my retirement was forced upon me by having multiple sclerosis, which came as a bit of a bolt from the blue. It means I can't do the job as I have always done it. I have thoroughly enjoyed running the school, but because I can't run it that way any more I decided to call it a day.

We've certainly been used to seeing you walking about the school all the time.
Yes, it's how you know what's going on - being in the action. It's a style of management the Americans call "Management by Walking About". It's very effective. Far too many managers hide themselves in their offices, pushing paper and so on. The secret of my success was being out and about - and available. Anyone could see me all the time.

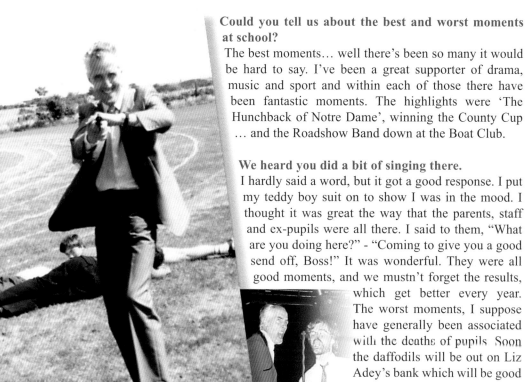

Could you tell us about the best and worst moments at school?
The best moments… well there's been so many it would be hard to say. I've been a great supporter of drama, music and sport and within each of those there have been fantastic moments. The highlights were 'The Hunchback of Notre Dame', winning the County Cup … and the Roadshow Band down at the Boat Club.

We heard you did a bit of singing there.
I hardly said a word, but it got a good response. I put my teddy boy suit on to show I was in the mood. I thought it was great the way that the parents, staff and ex-pupils were all there. I said to them, "What are you doing here?" - "Coming to give you a good send off, Boss!" It was wonderful. They were all good moments, and we mustn't forget the results, which get better every year. The worst moments, I suppose have generally been associated with the deaths of pupils. Soon the daffodils will be out on Liz Adey's bank which will be good to see, to remind us of a very nice young lady.

Keith Atkinson as cowboy and teddy boy.

124

What were the most serious and silliest things you've ever had to tell anyone off for?

Violence towards other pupils, threatening behaviour... The silliest thing I suppose is drinking on site. People really ought to have more sense. I remember one occasion when a lad came to school with a bottle of whisky from home. His punishment was to be dragged home by me. His mum opened the door and when I said he had been drinking she went absolutely wappy.

There's nothing more important than school discipline. You can't manage without it. You can be the most brilliant teacher but if you don't have any audience then it's no good

What motivated you to become a teacher?

I was aware that I was talented. I had a high work capacity. I was pretty bright and extremely fit. I thought I should use these gifts to help other people. I think some modern thinking has been counter to that – it's been about self, about money - even to the extent of exploiting people.

Teachers pay tribute to outgoing head

STAFF and pupils have paid tribute to the headteacher of Tuxford Comprehensive School, **Mr Keith Atkinson**, who has retired after 17 years at the school because of ill health.

Mr Atkinson (58) became head in 1978, shortly after the school became a comprehensive and he has seen the number of pupils rise from 739 with no sixth form to almost a thousand including 150 sixth-formers.

He started his teaching career at West Bridgford South County School in 1957, then gained a degree and a diploma in education at Durham University before becoming a teacher at Toot Hill Secondary School, Bingham.

He taught in Derbyshire

Mr Atkinson, of Newark Road, Southwell, told the Advertiser: "I was very sad to leave but I have got multiple sclerosis and can no longer be the up-front, energetic headteacher that such a successful school needs.

"I can look back on a successful career and I wish the next headteacher all the best."

A statement to parents on behalf of teachers at the school said: "He had a clear picture of the kind of active confident, well-motivated well-disciplined community

Appropriate transport for retirement: John Marshall's vintage bus.

What's fantastic is what happens here; we have a school which takes everybody from the non-reader to the very bright and we help them to push on to what they are capable of.

I'd like to have had more time – but, as they say, quit while you're a Head!

What qualities would you look for in your successor?

That is an extremely difficult question, because it pre-supposes that I knew what I was doing. I suppose honesty, integrity, openness, commitment to the common good. I'd want to ask certain questions actually.

Such as?

Do you want your own parking place? - a simple question, but a good indicator. Anyone who thinks he or she should have a reserved parking place has got the wrong attitude.

Do you expect the secretaries to make you a cup of coffee? - I always made my own. For a long time I didn't have an office, but it didn't matter to me. Some managers are preoccupied with the trappings - the parking place, the carpet… These things don't matter a damn. What matters is your commitment.

It will be difficult to find someone as devoted to the school as you.

The problem will be thinking "That's how it's done" and trying to find a match. I suggest the best idea is to get somebody different - a different view.

What has been the secret of your success?

I think it lies in being able to inspire people. It's done by demonstrating commitment and enthusiasm – and I have enjoyed every minute.

Keith Atkinson at Buckingham Palace

A letter from Mrs Celia Atkinson to Mr Steve Smith

Dear Steve

Thank you very much for your good wishes following Keith's mention in the New Year's Honours. We have been overwhelmed and delighted by the warmth of the response. Keith expected to take some stick in the light of his consistent and strongly expressed views on the government, particularly its education policies, but the personal support he has had has been wonderful. One of the unexpected bonuses of the award for us has been the pleasure it appears to have given other people. We have appreciated this more than we can say.

We had a memorable day on the 11th of February. Both the girls were able to be with us, which made it extra special; Juliet came over from Paris, having accumulated enough extra flexi-time to take a long weekend, and Clare had a half-day from her job with Barnet. We stayed overnight at a hotel near Regents Park, and drove to the Palace on Tuesday morning. We joined the queue of cars outside the main gates whilst the police gave our car a thorough going-over, and went over to take photos of Keith in full morning dress regalia in front of the gates - a truly impressive sight! The Japanese tourists clearly thought so, as they rushed over to have photos taken with him - obviously Jimmy Hill/Bruce Forsyth are really big in Japan.

The operation inside the Palace is incredibly smooth and efficient, and you are treated with great charm and courtesy from the moment you park your modest car among the Rolls, Bentleys and enormous stretch limos in the Quadrangle to the time you take your last photo and drive back into the real world. Celia was very taken with the beautiful guards decoratively on duty in sparkling white breeches and jackets, shining breastplates and helmets, and thigh-length leather boots. Definitely on the Christmas list.

The investiture is in the ballroom, and Keith was in for a surprise. His original citation had been 'for services to young people in Nottinghamshire and to the sport of rowing'. The Lord Steward reads out the name of each recipient, together with the achievement for which s/he is being decorated. Keith was astonished and delighted to hear 'for services to the Tuxford Comprehensive School and to rowing in Nottinghamshire'. I don't think his feet touched the floor as he went forward to meet H.M. who asked if Tuxford is a comprehensive school! Nothing could have made his day more completely. Whether it had anything to do with Tuxford being named in the Ofsted report as one of only 63 secondary schools in the country to have received excellent reports in the 1995-6 round of inspections we can only speculate. It certainly made a most rewarding end to his eighteen years at Tuxford.

We have had a great time with the wonderful farewells from Tuxford and now this special occasion which went so beautifully, and we are both grateful to everyone who made it all so memorable.

Celia

● Keith Atkinson collects his MBE at Buckingham Palace

Former head's honour for school success

TUXFORD Comprehensive was given recognition for its excellent performance when the school's former head received his MBE.

Keith Atkinson, who retired last year after 18 years as Head of Tuxford, received his MBE from the Queen on February 11.

There was a suprise in store for him when the Lord Steward announced, as the achievement for which he had been decorated, was 'for services to the Tuxford Comprehensive School and to rowing in Nottinghamshire.' The original citation had read 'for services to young people in Nottinghamshire, and to the sport of rowing.'

Keith said: "I could hardly believe my ears. I was absolutely delighted, and felt proud to be at Buckingham Palace representing this fine and outstandingly successful school."

Tuxford was one of only sixty three secondary schools in the country named recently by Ofsted as having received excellent reports in the 1995—6 inspections.

Extract from the *Retford Times* - 20 February 1997

Letter from Mr Atkinson's wife to Steve Smith at Tuxford School.

The 2007 Building

Part of the Bassetlaw PFI Project

During Mr Atkinson's latter years as headteacher it became apparent that the school's buildings were inadequate for three basic reasons: many parts were old and dilapidated, rooms – especially in lower school - were often too small in area to take large classes of older children and there were not enough teaching areas, changing rooms, toilets, etc for the increasing numbers of students being admitted. The head's reports to the Governing Body sometimes express exasperation and sometimes incredulity:

"The barn roof is being improved as is the interior but a long term replacement strategy is badly needed." (1)

"Through the Tuxford Recreational Association the school is attempting to gain use of the field behind Gilbert Avenue – unused for the past fifteen years! ...Demand for places at Tuxford School and the increasing numbers staying on in full-time education are putting pressure on our accommodation. By next September we will need AT LEAST two extra full sized general purpose classrooms. The Government promised help for successful schools in its pre-election rhetoric – I have written to Mr Patten asking him to honour his party's pledge." (2)

"The double classroom has still not been delivered... In addition it has been found that the electricity feed into school is inadequate to support new rooms and a new cable will have to be laid. The recent rains have highlighted the inadequacy of the roads and pathways around the school and major investment is needed in the basic infrastructure. The main hall floor has been replaced. The Authority contributed nothing to this project... Farmer Bett has refused to sell the field at the back of the school, despite an offer above the rate for agricultural land." (3)

"The point has been made many times that the popularity of Tuxford School has resulted in the total overload of its infrastructure. Within two years I believe that numbers will exceed 1000... A top priority must be to develop another area of the school grounds simply to spread numbers wider on the site. Plans have been submitted to expand around the RoSLA block." (4)

In 1995 school budgets were reduced. Tuxford's budget was cut by £98,000 so development projects were halted. In the same term it was revealed that the school was officially full – or overflowing, in fact, as it was 139% capacity. In a hostile financial climate it was clear that little money could be expected from county to improve the accommodation so senior managers took the view that self-help was needed. Governors and the community were consulted to see whether there was the necessary support for a bid for funding from the national lottery (which had held its first draw on 19th November 1994). Parent governor Ian Atkinson, a district councillor and tireless advocate of community development, was recruited together with parish council and county council representatives. From their deliberations came a plan to seek funding for a sport and arts building to have shared use by the school and community. Graham Curry, head of PE, attended a meeting on 20 July 1995 together with office manager Joyce Hallam and the headteacher. An extract from the minutes reveals the issues and proposed funding for the project:

Backing plans for sports hall

PROPOSALS to develop a new sports hall in Tuxford won important backing on Monday.

Nottinghamshire's education committee welcomed an idea by Tuxford Recreational Association to build a new sports hall at Tuxford School and agreed in principle to lease the land to the association so the project can go ahead.

A report to the committee described the existing sports hall at the school as dilapidated and of limited value to the school. The idea is for it to be demolished to make way for a new hall with changing facilities.

The association was formed to explore ways of developing sports facilities in Tuxford that could be used by the school during the day and the community outside school hours. The school is backing the plan.

The scheme is only in its initial planning stage but the likely cost is put between £350,000 and £1½m.

The association asked the committee to consider leasing the land at a nominal rent because it does not think the scheme could go ahead without the subsidy.

The association intends to seek grants from a variety of sources including the Football Trust, the Rural Community Council and the National Lottery and raise its own cash towards the project.

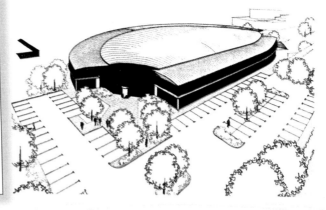

Reproduced courtesy of the *Newark Advertiser.* 17 Nov 1995.

Proposed multi-purpose leisure and learning centre - 1995/96.

"The first essential was to clarify the position regarding the purchase of a 2.4 (acre) parcel of land known as Betts Field and for which a sum of money has been offered... Mr Curry visited the Garibaldi School as they had undertaken a similar project and had received 'matched' funding to facilitate the project... Bagguley Construction, the contractors used by Garibaldi had been to inspect the Tuxford site and make suggestions regarding i planning permission, ii alternative vehicular / disabled access (off Marnham Road), iii the most cost effective method of providing an indoor sports area...

"Funding applications had been requested from the Football Trust, who were likely to help specifically with the changing rooms, the Rural Community Council, the National Lottery would need to be approached at a later date when firmer time scales could be set... Application forms have been received from the Foundation for Sport and Arts... We hope to make a list of businesses within the catchment area with a view to approaching them. Finally, should we manage to raise at least 50% of the money ourselves from funding agencies, it would seem

Reproduced courtesy of the *Newark Advertiser.* 15 Nov 1996.

£1m scheme unveiled

DESIGNS showing how a proposed £1m leisure and learning community centre in Tuxford would look went on show on Friday.

Collingham architect and energy consultant Ursula Bradwell has drawn up the plans, which are on display in a shop in the village centre.

She is pictured (right) with Mrs Marilyn McCarthy, who represents Tuxford on Bassetlaw District Council; Mrs Carole Lowe, editor of the Tuxfordian community newspaper and Mr Ian Atkinson, chairman of the Tuxford Toward 2000 project.

Mrs McCarthy said: "This is the latest stage of the project and it is particularly interesting because local people can get an idea on how the centre would look."

The project would provide indoor and outdoor leisure facilities and a learning centre behind Tuxford School. The idea is for the centre to be developed in stages between next year and the year 2000.

Tuxford has a population of around 2,600 and several thousand people live in many small communities around it.

The learning project would allow them to travel to the Tuxford centre to take advantage of computer link-ups with other colleges, rather than have to travel greater distances for education.

National Lottery money will be sought.

reasonable to approach Notts. LEA to ask them to match that figure." (5)

Keith Atkinson was already ill at this stage, but newly promoted deputy headteacher Beth Soule - Acting Headteacher from February to September 1996 - became an enthusiastic supporter. By November 1995 the basic proposal was ready. The Education Committee, at a meeting on 13 November 1995, agreed to lease school land to the Project for joint community use as the neighbouring farmer continued to resist a sale of land. The Toward 2000 proposal document revealed this and gave the following details of the building that school managers were advocating as well as some of their reasoning:

"The school's gym, barn and changing rooms were built for a secondary modern school of 360. Tuxford is a successful comprehensive school of nearly 1000. There is urgent need of more land, community facilities, a sports pavilion, upgraded PE facilities and a multi media block…

"It is envisaged that the work will encompass the following…: demolish existing barn, redevelop pitches and courts to provide good all weather outdoor playing surfaces for football, tennis, etc…, an indoor sports hall, changing facilities, multi functional dance/drama/recreational rooms…, a multi media and open learning technology resource centre." (6)

Ian Atkinson was chairing the project by now and Joyce Hallam was doing much of the administrative work. Community surveys were conducted and an architect, Ursula Bradwell from Collingham, was commissioned to draw up outline plans. A year after the basic proposal was published the outline plans were ready and the Newark Advertiser report of 15 November 1996 revealed that one million pounds would be sought for the project. (7) Mr Pickering had taken up his post as Tuxford School's third headteacher at the start of the term and he fully supported the initiative. To increase the prospect of lottery funding the school needed to establish a commitment to the local community so the summer 1997 edition of Tuxford Topics revealed that a preliminary lottery bid had secured some funding to promote professional arts events and also that from September a Learning Café would be available after school for activities such as chess, computer access, reading in the library and drama. (8)

In the spring 1998 edition Mrs Soule wrote: "…but now the real crunch has to be faced. We have to raise 25% of the funds ourselves, and that is a considerable sum of money." (9)

In December 1998 Beth Soule left to become headteacher of Claydon High School near Ipswich. With her departure some of the drive

New school on old site

A £15m SCHEME to demolish and rebuild Tuxford School is scheduled for completion by 2006.

The project has been approved by Nottinghamshire County Council, clearing the way for building work to begin in two years.

It is part of a £111m project to restructure secondary education in Bassetlaw.

The work at Tuxford has been included in the £55m first phase that is due to be implemented over the next four years.

Expected

The headteacher, Mr Chris Pickering, said: "The school buildings do not fulfil their requirements.

"The new school will be state-of-the-art and as good as anywhere else in the country.

"It is something we have been fighting for for a long time and now it does not seem to be a matter of if it goes ahead, but when."

It is expected that the new school will be built on the part of the present playing fields.

Pupils will continue to be taught in the current premises while building work continues.

When the new school is complete the old buildings will be demolished.

The scheme will be paid for by the private sector.

The county council will then make annual payments to use the buildings.

The original central block of Tuxford Comprehensive School was opened in 1958 to house 350 pupils.

More blocks were added as pupil numbers grew to 1,100.

The review of Bassetlaw's secondary education looked at ways of reducing surplus places, improving facilities for 16 to18-year-olds and tackling the poor state of school buildings.

Phase one also includes plans for a shake-up of secondary schools in Retford, including the possible closure of King Edward VI and Ordsall Hall Schools and the replacement of Elizabethan High School.

Reproduced courtesy of the *Newark Advertiser*. 17 May 2002

went out of the project – after all it was getting very close to the new millennium which it was supposed to mark. There was no need for governor Ian Atkinson to feel despondent as other projects he led bore fruit such as establishment of the Mine of Information in Tuxford and a new community centre, Millennium Hall, in Dunham-on-Trent. An alternative method of funding public projects was becoming more common and this source was, eventually, to lead to the construction of the new school.

Private Finance Initiatives (PFI) began under the government of John Major in 1992 and after the 1997 general election. PFI continued and, indeed, expanded under Tony Blair. Under the scheme hospitals, schools, prisons and other public facilities would be built and managed by companies on contract to government or local authorities. For a fixed period annual fees and payments would be made to the companies so long as they maintained standards of service. The Newark Advertiser of 19 October 2001 revealed that the county council would prepare a PFI bid before Christmas and would include a plan to rebuild Tuxford School: "The county admits that demolishing the school would remove some of the worst school accommodation in the county." (10) Nottinghamshire duly applied to the government in December 2001 - for £114 million PFI "credits" - to upgrade secondary schools in Retford and Worksop areas. The Tuxford building would cost £15.5 million. Mr Pickering had played a very active part in lobbying the LEA, ministers and the local M.P. prior to the bid being made so he awaited the outcome with interest.

The bid was partially successful so either the Retford or the Worksop scheme could go ahead whilst another bid would have to go in for the rest of the Bassetlaw project. A meeting of the county council cabinet on Wednesday May 8th 2002 decided that Retford and Tuxford would go ahead as the proposed phase one. As soon as Notts County Council confirmed

Plans for new school building taking shape

WORK on a new building to replace the existing Tuxford School could start as soon as next year.

Outline plans for the new school appeared before Notts County Council on Tuesday.

The plans show the building will be located on the current school playing fields with a new access from Marnham Road.

The work is part of the education review of the area which will also see two new schools built in Retford by 2006.

Much of the current Tuxford School was built in the early 1960s and education chiefs are keen to see the old building replaced with a new state-of-the-art facility.

And headteacher Chris Pickering said the new building would compliment the school's achievements.

"We are finally going to have a building to match the school's performance," he said.

Several plans for the new building are set to be drawn up and Mr Pickering said he and other members of staff would play a role in its final design.

"Essentially we want all classrooms to be under one roof but if other designs are put forward then obviously they will be looked at," he said.

"We want good PE facilities, a sports hall and a gym, as well as state-of-the-art ICT facilities."

He said work on the new school could begin next autumn and would be completed for September 2006.

The current building, which includes a tower block, will eventually be demolished.

Reproduced courtesy of the *Retford Times*. 24 July 2003.

that Tuxford School was to be rebuilt Chris Pickering wrote to parents to tell them the good news. "We are absolutely delighted," he commented. "We are extremely excited at the prospect of having buildings and facilities of the highest standard – to match the quality of education that we already provide."

The county PFI team was busy during the rest of 2002 in preparing to invite "expressions of interest" from finance and building consortia and in setting up an administration base in Worksop. Headteachers meanwhile were arranging visits to other PFI schools, and consulting staff and community representatives regarding features they would like to see in the design. Ian Atkinson who had been so active in the Toward 2000 project was consulted to see whether the original aim of providing community sports facilities could be achieved. Room data sheets and design priorities were to be prepared; deputy head Geoff Lloyd and former school business manager Glenn Turner took on the job of collation.

Each school's Design Priority Statement had to be prepared for the competing building consortia by March 2003. Tuxford School stipulated, among others, the following design features: use of as much natural light as possible, solid brick or block walls and a pitched roof, avoidance of dark 'hiding places', clear panels in all classroom doors, a compact building of two or three storeys, all areas to be reached from indoors – no need to go outside - but alternative routes to be available by going out, wide corridor areas to include space for lockers, an attractive and distinctive reception area with exhibition space at the centre of a support services suite, a staffroom to hold 120 people and a kitchenette, electronic

door locking from a central location as a security measure, an outdoor dining area adjacent to the dining room, 130 staff parking places plus other spaces for sixth form students and visitors, adequate parking for 20 buses. Undesirable features – to be avoided at all costs – were also identified: an 'off the shelf' building, the appearance of an office block, flat roofs, poor acoustics and sub-standard materials. (11)

Ten potential bidders for the Bassetlaw contract identified themselves, but by 26th September 2003 when formal Invitations to Negotiate were issued there was a shortlist of three. Many visits were paid to schools by the bidders and county architect Peter Price attended all meetings as an adviser. The deadline for receipt of designs was 16 January 2004 and after that the three groups were asked to clarify issues. The following response from the Balfour Beatty consortium – the group eventually awarded the contract – appears to satisfy the requirement that designs should not be 'off the shelf' concepts:

"The Private Finance Initiative is being used extensively to replace large numbers of schools

Mr Pickering paying a site visit.

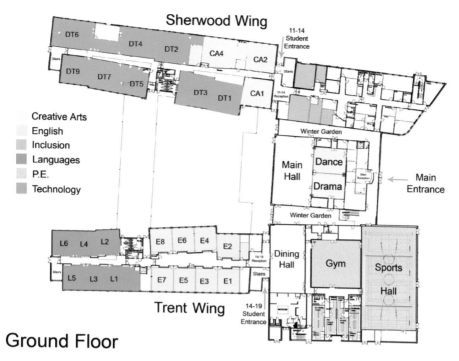

Sherwood Wing

Ground Floor

Trent Wing

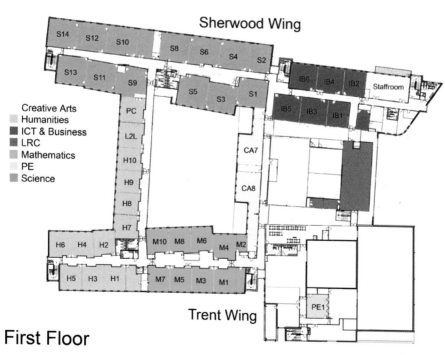

Sherwood Wing

First Floor

Trent Wing

An early artist's impression of the main entrance. The viewing gallery in the sports hall - where the windows can be seen next to the logo - was not built because the resources for it were put into classrooms.

from the late '60s and early '70s, which were built using repetitive designs and construction systems, and which are now reaching the end of their useful lives. This systematic approach to school design is now generally disliked by modern educators, not just for its technical obsolescence, but for its implication that school ethos, spirit, students and curriculum are uniform and interchangeable. Independent expression of school ethos is seen as a positive, and the concept of individuality being expressed at each of the project schools has formed a key element of Transform Schools' approach to the design process." (12)

The design for Tuxford was a two storey building divided into two wings running at an angle from each other. "Bridges" were to connect the wings at first floor level so the shape would be that of a capital A or a pair of dividers. The main entrance was to be at the apex with wood cladding on the external wall to the right of the entrance (behind which the senior managers and administration team were to be based) and a light coloured modern finish on the left of the entrance (covering the sports hall). The entrance was to have no inner lobby with inner and outer doors to retain heat (similar to the one in the 1958 building); instead doors would open directly onto reception. Hot air blowers set in the ceiling were intended to provide a curtain of heat to keep visitors warm even on the coldest day.

In a July submission Transform Schools set out to explain how it had complied with schools' design priorities. The reception is mentioned: "The deep plan area containing the main assembly hall and large non-timetabled spaces are lit and naturally vented through the introduction of two winter gardens. The school's main entrance through the deep plan design then provides the controllable large central foyer space through which all of the various functions of the school building (are) accessed,... Circulation was clearly identified in the vision statement as a key concern of the school who requested the design to be as open and as free flowing as possible. The design responds by providing a race track system where pupils can circulate freely around the school without retracing their footsteps – much of the circulation is through two storey atrium areas to provide transparency." (13) This appears to suggest that the reception area was seen as a primary access route to all areas.

Balfour Beatty / Transform Schools was awarded the contract on 15th September 2004. Unfortunately, the signing of the contract was delayed whilst contractor and government clarified issues. Governors Mick Jones and Richard Bartholomew signed for Tuxford School during the Easter holiday 2005 but the main signing occurred at Edinburgh in July. Although work on the new Tuxford School began almost immediately, the planned completion date had to be put back from September 2006 to February 2007. Dave Cook, former teacher of technology but now Budget Manager, provided the school's primary liaison with the construction team. Deputy General Manager for Transform Schools, Gary Fisher, was a frequent visitor to the school to meet with Mr Cook or Mr Pickering. Tuxford professional photographer Dick Makin was commissioned to record the building process as construction proceeded apace: the site was levelled by the start of August and much of the steel framework was in place when the new term began in September. Most of the building was completed by November 2006, but the fitting out continued until the official handover on 26th February 2007. Although demolition of the old school did not start for a few months it was completed in June 2007.

Ten years after Beth Soule had been facing "the crunch" of raising a huge sum of money for a new sport and art centre, a new building had emerged that would have been beyond her wildest imagining at the time. The original building had missed the fiftieth anniversary of its construction by three weeks because work on it had started in July 1957. Construction methods for the new building were not that much different from those employed fifty years before: mass produced components were used to save time and money; steel frames were hidden in a shell formed from different

July 2005.

Sept 2005.

Oct 2005.

April 2006.

Mr Pickering's School

Reproduced courtesy of the *Newark Advertiser.* 2 Mar 2007.

N.B. Dominic was present to take part in a video recording, not as the last to leave.

Ready to learn in new school

By Emma Pietras

THE keys to the new £15m Tuxford School were handed to the head on Monday.

Mr Geoff Lloyd received the keys from Mr Gary Fisher, of Transform Schools, which was chosen by Nottinghamshire County Council to rebuild the school.

Those at the ceremony included Mr John Pepper (63) of Henton Road, Edwinstowe, who was the first pupil to arrive at the old school building when it opened in 1958.

Also there were Tamsin Bickley (16) Aaron Ellis (16) and Dominic O'Connell (14) who were the final three pupils to leave.

Mr Lloyd said: "It's taken longer than we thought to move all the boxes but it has been worth it. This school has fantastic facilities and will offer better opportunities for our pupils."

Computer

The new school, on Marnham Road, has been built on part of the playing fields of the old school, which will be demolished.

Facilities include nine science labs, four computer rooms, a gym, a sports hall and a learning resource centre with lap tops for more flexible learning.

The 1,300 pupils were due to return today for an orientation day to allow them to get used to the building before lessons start on Monday.

After the hand-over Mr Pepper was given a tour of the new premises.

"We thought that when we moved into the old school that it was fantastic but it doesn't compare to this," Mr Pepper said.

He couldn't believe the amount of facilities that young people had today and hoped they looked after the new school.

external materials and finishes for the sake of aesthetic appeal. The old building had gone, but the ideas behind it lived on. More importantly, the school had enough space to thrive and expand.

Sources

1   *Headteacher's Report to Governing Body September 1991*, Keith Atkinson, Tuxford School Archive Papers, unpublished

2   *Headteacher's Report to Governing Body September 1992*, Keith Atkinson, Tuxford School Archive Papers, unpublished

3   *Headteacher's Report to Governing Body September 1993*, Keith Atkinson, Tuxford School Archive Papers, unpublished

4   *Headteacher's Report to Governing Body February 1995*, Keith Atkinson, Tuxford School Archive Papers, unpublished

5   *Minutes of meeting held on 20 July 1995*, Toward 2000 Project

6   *Toward 2000 Community Leisure and Learning*, Tuxford School and Tuxford Recreation Association, November 1995

7   *£1m scheme unveiled, Newark Advertiser,* 15 November 1996

8   *Various news items, Tuxford Topics,* Summer 1997

9   *Editorial,* Tuxford Topics, Spring 1998

10   *School rebuild agreed,* Newark Advertiser, 19 October 2001

11   *Tuxford School Design Priority Statement* (March 2003), Tuxford School Archive Papers, unpublished, 2003

12   *Responses to Questions following the Design Presentation*, Transform Schools, February 2004

13   *Invitation to Negotiate Submission 2*, Transform Schools, July 2004

History in the Making
Article from 2006 Year Book

Our Year Group is the one that witnessed the most significant event in Tuxford School's history for almost fifty years. We saw the old buildings becoming ever more tired and dilapidated and at the same time we saw the new building rise. At first the new school was just a steel skeleton, but gradually the floors and walls were added – and we soon realised that it was literally over-shadowing the old buildings. Our familiar long-serving school was being deprived of daylight so that it was looking even more shabby in contrast to the bold new edifice arising before our eyes.

There is no doubt that a new school was necessary. As the school population grew we were operating from a village of "mobile classrooms" and trekking long distances – often in pouring rain – from one lesson to the next. We were expected to take the long route around the back of the school to get from Maths to IT, but sometimes opted for the excitement of breaking the rules: a walk past not only parked staff cars but also the staff room to the accompanying angry sound of displeased teachers shouting, "Oi, where do you think you are going?" The years had not been kind to some of the buildings. The "tower block" (a brilliant example of exaggeration) had developed a slight but discernible lean. The drama studio had become damp and smelly. The "barn" was dark and bristling with sharp surfaces to damage soft bodies. The hall floor had to be replaced twice in our time because the quad flooded and the drains could not cope. Lots of classrooms had leaking roofs. The dining areas were far too small and they had the worst furniture in the school so we were seldom tempted to linger. There weren't enough toilets or lockers, the lights down the drive shed little illumination on the narrow uneven footpath, some outside areas became traps for wind-blown litter – the list of faults in the old school grows ever longer.

But there were lots of good memories of the old place too. Not only will we remember the daffodils lining the drive in spring and the hens roaming the paths and car parks, but also the excellent playing field, the many trees, the picnic tables where we could sit during breaks on warm days. Every part of the building was modified and improved to create extra space. The reception area looked impressive with its staff photos, display cases and certificates. Everywhere were colourful displays of work. The building was a maze – but there was always a spot we could call our own, where we could meet our friends and escape the crowd.

The actual building process was fascinating. Every day we could look out to see the changes as they occurred: the heavy equipment used to move earth or lift girders, the scaffolding giving way to completed walls. Loss of access to the field during construction was restricting and the staff lost one third of their car park too. However, we were there to witness it all: we saw history being made. We knew and respected the old building and we could admire the new one before it was occupied. Exciting changes happened to Tuxford School in our time there – and we will never forget them.

On Task, On Target *The story of the first fifty years of Tuxford School*

Thoughts on Accommodation
by Chris Pickering
From 'Building On Success'
A School Marketing Team Film, 2007

Ten years ago I think there were just a few students below one thousand in this school. I think Post 16 there were about one hundred and fifty. The latest count this September – September 2006 – shows that we have almost 1300 students in the school and of these 1300, 244 are Post 16.

In the ten years that I have been at Tuxford it has been quite obvious that the quality of the buildings has been degenerating year by year as the student numbers have risen. Consequently we are tightly packed inside the building. There is not enough space: classrooms are small, corridors are very narrow. Coupled with this, the physical state of the building doesn't produce the optimum environment for learning - the roofs leak, the window frames are rotting, that sort of thing – so it is vital for us as a school that we can move into a building where that environment is there.

At one point we were named 'Mobile City' within the Authority because our numbers culminated in about fourteen mobile classrooms as we stand at the moment – and of course that is far too many. There is far too much movement in and out of the building, making the building filthy, mucky: the mobiles are situated around the perimeter so the youngsters have to cross muddy areas. Get rid of the mobiles, into the new school, purpose-built, where everybody can move from one part of the school to another under cover with no need to be going in and out of the building, it is going to be absolutely superb.

We have maintained the current building as best we can. We have tried to extend where we have been able to afford it, we have tried to refurbish where we have been able to afford it, and significant changes have taken place over the last ten years, but they have not got to the root of the problem. The LEA was very keen to listen. They even had plans drawn up to refurbish the old building on the current site, but part way through that process it became apparent that the large amounts of money required would not be forthcoming unless something different happened. To refurbish this building would probably cost more than to build a new one. At the end of the day the building is tired, the building has had its day and the new facilities are long overdue.

First discussions about PFI probably took place about five to seven years ago and it

Part of the "Mobile City".

has taken a good five years to get from the initial decision within the council to pursue the PFI route to seeing the school built: quite a long time but it has flown.

We thought at the beginning there would be a danger that we would be presented with a school that we would have to work in, but that has not proved to be the case. We have been involved right from the start. Three or four years ago we were able to produce a priority design statement informing the architects of every aspect of the culture, the philosophy and the ethos of the school and how we would like it reflected in the design of the building. We have been involved right the way through the design and build process with architects, with builders, with officers of the LEA. Apart from a few things the school that has appeared now that we will occupy in March reflects one hundred per cent of our requirements and requests. For example, we wanted it to be a school where students could have outdoor shelter so there are bridges within the design and there is shelter under two bridges where there are classrooms above.

In the early days we had to work with three different companies or consortia. They put their bids in and then they were short listed down. We had to work on three sets of everything and that was a time consuming process. We had to contribute to a day when presentations were made by the three companies. That 'Evaluation Day' was an important part of deciding which bidder won the contract. We had a big say in that and I have to say our choice was the one that won it.

School rebuild agreed

AN AMBITIOUS scheme to demolish and rebuild Tuxford School should go ahead, Nottinghamshire County Council decided on Wednesday.

The central block was built in 1958 for 350 pupils, with more blocks added over the years to accommodate 1,110 pupils.

The county admits that demolishing the school would remove some of the worst school accommodation in the county. It would be replaced on the existing site.

The scheme is part of a major reorganisation of education in Bassetlaw.

Improving facilities for 16 to 18-year-olds will be assessed but the county agrees Tuxford should retain its sixth form.

The reorganisation, including the Tuxford work, will be paid for through a private finance initiative.

The next step will be to prepare this bid, estimated at more than £50m, for Government consideration in time for Christmas.

A timescale for reorganisation work is still to be decided.

Science teacher Rhona Ward and deputy head Dave Cottom sitting in the amphitheatre area.

Reproduced courtesy of the *Newark Advertiser*.
19 Oct 2001.

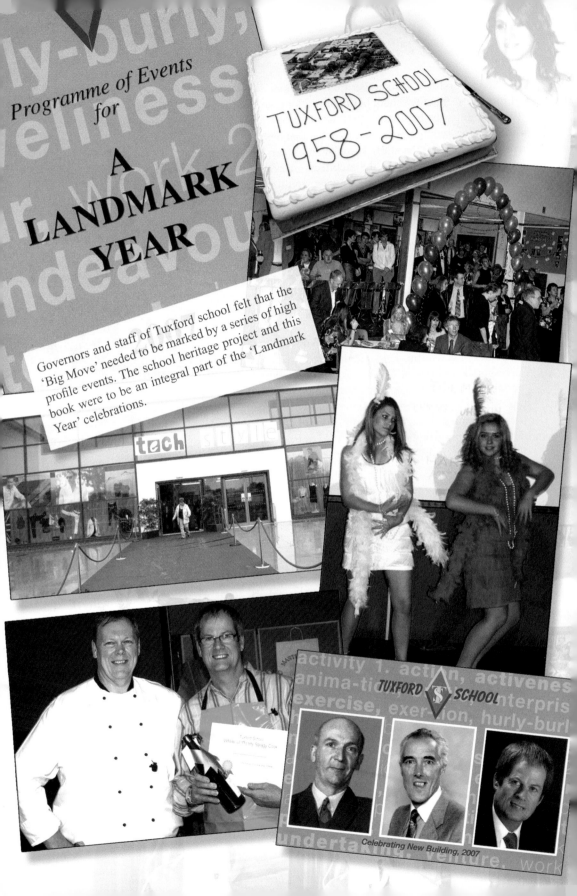

Programme of Events for

A LANDMARK YEAR

TUXFORD SCHOOL 1958 - 2007

Governors and staff of Tuxford school felt that the 'Big Move' needed to be marked by a series of high profile events. The school heritage project and this book were to be an integral part of the 'Landmark Year' celebrations.

Celebrating New Building, 2007

CRATES, SNAGS AND REJOICING
Tuxford Topics, Summer Term 2007

"We don't want to do that for another fifty years!" That was the general verdict after normal work routines were established in the new school. Remember what it was like when you last moved house then multiply all the chaos, insecurity, excitement and exhaustion by ten and you might have some idea how the staff were feeling at the end of 'The Big Move.'

The new classrooms were wonderful – but the heating didn't work properly at first. All 4000 crates arrived safely, but sometimes there was not enough storage space in new offices. Everywhere was freshly decorated, clean and airy, but there were no noticeboards. In the end, the Tuxford sense of humour and goodwill saw us through – but there were moments of disappointment, frustration and discomfort as we settled in.

Final lessons in the old building were held on Tuesday, February 13th. During the following three days staff packed and labelled 4000 plastic crates for removal firm Harrow Green to take to the new school. After half term staff were able to unpack before students arrived on the Friday (March 2nd) to learn the layout of room and lockers.

The first major event in the new school was the Governors' Reception for staff and key PFI stakeholders on Monday 5th March. Chair of Governors, Mick Jones, officially welcomed staff to their new workbase and also presented small gifts to some of the people who played a significant role in creating the new school or in the move.

On Tuesday 13th March, Headteacher Chris Pickering hosted a reception for all staff working in our eleven feeder primary schools. Tours of the building were arranged so that the visitors could tell primary classes what they could look forward to when they move into Year 7.

Our phone number has been restored, the building "snags" are being fixed and noticeboards are going up – so the new school feels more like home with every passing day.

Mr Terry White
School Press Officer

VIRUS DECIMATES SCHOOL CLASSES

by **James Peck**
james.peck@retfordtimes.co.uk

Illness leaves up to third of pupils missing

A VIRUS causing sickness and dizziness has swept through schools in the Retford area, decimating pupil and staff attendance.

More than 30 per cent of Tuxford School's 1,300 pupils - 400 students - were absent this week as the bug took hold.

Elizabethan High School and Retford Oaks both reported 20 per cent of pupils affected.

Despite the numbers of people affected, no school has had to close.

Parents are advised to ensure sick children rest, drink plenty of fluids and are symptom-free for at least 24 hours before returning to school.

"Even though 30 per cent sounds a high number, the school and staff have coped well," said Tuxford School's press officer Terry White.

"There weren't entire classes disappearing, it was a few pupils in each class.

SCHOOL'S OUT: Attendances at the area's secondary schools have been hit by a virus affecting up to a third of pupils at one time

"Only one or two teachers were off due to the bug this week so generally the school was fine," he added.

Elizabethan's Lynn French said her school will be monitoring the situation.

"Obviously 20 per cent of 1,200 pupils is a large figure," said Elizabethan High School's Head, Lynn French.

"This is a nasty virus that has affected children's attendance but we have not had to close and will monitor the situation closely," she added.

Mrs French said some staff are ill but most remain untouched by the bug.

Retford Oaks Head David Rich praised his staff and said parents were taking a proactive approach to the illness.

"The staff have been brilliant," he said.

"They have coped admirably during the virus and we have not sent children home - parents who think their children are ill have generally kept them at home."

Mr Rich added that staff have been filling in for those few teachers hit by the illness.

Reproduced courtesy of the *Retford Times*. 9 Feb 2006

SCHOOL BUS IN ICY ROAD CRASH

Calls for gritting to cover all routes

by **Sally Clark**
sally.clark@retfordtimes.co.uk

Reproduced courtesy of the *Retford Times*. 11 Dec 2003.

PARENTS are calling for school routes to be gritted after a bus carrying pupils slid off the road and crashed into trees near Upton.

The accident happened yesterday (Wednesday) morning as the bus was collecting pupils to take them to Tuxford School.

The 78-seater double-decker appeared to have slid off the road at a bend and came to rest leaning into the ditch.

None of the 61 pupils on board the bus was injured although some were distressed.

Nigel Ball's daughter was on the bus and he said the road was very icy.

"I received a distressed phone call from my daughter saying the bus had crashed.

"I went to get her and the road was like a sheet of black ice.

"The driver didn't stand a chance."

Mr Ball said he realised the route was a minor road but felt that as a school bus route gritting should be carried out.

Customer Services Manager for the Highways Department Dick Statham said the county policy is to grit all A ... roads and most C ...

Mr Statham said if a large number of school buses use a route then gritting considered.

"But quite often it is just one bus using the route," he added.

A spokesman for Kettlewells, who operate the Tuxford bus said: "As a company we feel that all roads of whatever category, as bus or coach routes, should be gritted."

One parent said there had been concerns about overcrowded buses on this route.

A Notts County Council spokesman said there were 80 children assigned to the route and a 78 seater bus was usually used or a 74 seater.

"Obviously not every child travels every day but when they do some children will have to stand," she said.

"This is legal providing it is within the standing limit for that particular bus.

"This is not encouraged but sometimes it has to happen when every child travels."

Headteacher Chris Pickering said the school was thankful that no-one was injured.

PUPILS from Tuxford Comprehensive school with Bill Oddie at High Marnham power station on Friday. The pupils are, from the left, Joanna Farr, Emma Hudson, Karen Hutchinson, Samantha Welton, and Clare Buttrick, all aged 12.

TV celebrity charmed by twitchers

CELEBRITY conservationist Bill Oddie met children from Tuxford School on Friday to talk about the passion that now takes up most of his time.

The former Goodie was at the Eastern Generation power station at High Marnham to talk about his love of bird watching and his work with the Royal Society for the Protection of Birds.

He is spearheading a nationwide campaign, sponsored by Eastern Generation, to achieve better protection for wildlife locations that have been designated Sites of Special Scientific Interest.

The campaign is called Land For Life and its connection with High Marnham Power Station lies in the fact that there are about 60 different bird species on the site, as well as a number of rare plants.

Bill Oddie said: "A lot of my best bird watching has been in SSIs and conservation areas like this. They are the nation's wildlife equivalent of the crown jewels."

He recounted some of the more memorable and bizarre incidents that had happened during his worldwide travels in pursuit of bird watching, including searching the rain forests of New Guinea in darkness and hunting for the rare capercaillie in the forests of Scotland.

Pupils from Tuxford were keen to meet him to talk about their survey of wildlife around the power station, carried out over the past couple of months.

He talked with them for nearly an hour and said he was pleased to see young people taking such a keen interest in wildlife conservation in the area. He was particularly impressed with the clarity and detail of their findings.

The children took part in a survey by the Lincoln RSPB, in conjunction with a school science project.

"We looked at the different species of birds and their characteristics and habitats," said Karen Hutchinson (12).

Liam Browne (12) said: "I didn't know that much about birds before doing this project but now I think I might like to take it up as a hobby in my spare time."

Questions

Bill Oddie spent time talking individually with the 11 children, aged 12 and 13, who worked on the project, and he was particularly interested to hear about an ostrich farm in Gamston owned by the parents of Joanna Farr (12). They have about 400 ostriches on 11 acres of farmland.

One of the children's main questions for Bill Oddie was what had made him want to become an ornithologist?

He said that as a young boy he used to spend hours in the countryside watching for birds and when he was ten his father bought him his first pair of binoculars.

"They were the best present I could ever have been bought," he said.

Reproduced courtesy of *Newark Advertiser.* 28 Nov 1998.

Mr Pickering's School

hen Mr Pickering was appointed on 17th April 96 Geoff Lloyd was already assistant head of the school and he remembered the occasion well: "I organised the appointment of the new head in 1996, but I didn't have a major role in terms of the decision-making. There was quite a lot of discussion going on behind the scenes and the local authority adviser was influential in advising the governors. Everyone was just looking for a head teacher to move the school forward. I can remember on the interview day asking someone, 'How is it going?' They said, 'Well nobody's coming out a clear winner' - and then Chris was interviewed."

As an indication of the qualities that impressed interviewers and led to Chris Pickering's appointment Mr Lloyd offered me this comparison of the two Tuxford headteachers he has worked with: "Keith could inspire by force of personality and Chris inspires by the innovation of his thinking.

"I think what we were looking for was a leader... We wanted a leader with a drive for success - that in part is what the Tuxford culture is - and that's what Chris is good at... I know people remember the differences - that Keith walked around, that he didn't want an office because he didn't have to do the paperwork whereas Chris is perhaps a bit more embedded in his office - but Chris does walk round and he often goes in the staff room. The key to success is a sense of humour within that determination: you've got to stand back and be able to laugh at yourself and the Tuxford sense of humour is still there. Both of them have an incredibly good sense of humour. They take their roles seriously and they want Tuxford to be the best

Tuxford Comprehensive pupil Paul Andrews and his helpers from the school's 'Kids Who Care' fundraising group notched up a staggering £1,000 from their Christmas raffle. Prizes for the raffle were secured from local businesses and the proceeds will go to the Sheffield Children's Hospital Neo-Natal Unit, which successfully treated Tuxford head teacher Chris Pickering's baby son Joshua. Pictured accepting a cheque from Paul is neo-natal nurse

Chris McLaughlin. Also present for the handover are Paul's Dad Pete and Chris Pickering with wife Kate and baby Joshua. Reproduced courtesy of the *Reford Times*. 23 Jan 1997.

school in the area, but they also know when to have a laugh and it's that balance." (1)

Soon after Mr Pickering took up his duties as head he had to focus on a family worry. Newly born son, Joshua, had health issues and needed an operation. It was performed at Sheffield Children's Hospital and all went well. The surprising consequence of the whole upsetting episode was that it revealed to Mr Pickering the quality of the school he had just joined. Fourteen year old Paul Andrews was so moved by the plight of the new headteacher's son that he determined to raise some money for the hospital. He started a group of fund-raisers called Kids Who Care and in January he was able to present neo-natal nurse Chris McLaughlin with a cheque for £1000 in the presence of Mr Pickering and family. The Retford Times was there to record the event. (2) Paul embodied the enterprise culture that had been established in the school under Mr Pickering's predecessor. He went on to raise a lot more money for good causes until he was tragically killed in a road crash. The annual charity fair held by the school is named after him.

Mr Pickering found himself in the Retford Times again in February 1997. The school had been named in the annual report from Ofsted as one of the highest performing schools from the previous cycle of inspections. (3) Subsequently, on October 23rd, junior education minister Estelle Morris visited the school to present a good schools award.

Mr Pickering's headship to date has been marked by many achievements and presentations. If we were to revive the image of the school's history as a journey then Mr Pickering encountered a few tricky moments in woodland at the start (budgetary constraints) but soon

A school inspector calls to discover class distinction

Praise for setting standards

☐ Head of Tuxford School, above, Mr Chris Pickering helps Helen

FIVE Newark area schools have proved they are among the best in the country. They have earned praise in the annual report of Her Majesty's Chief Inspector of Schools in England.

Primary, middle and nursery schools were chosen for their high standards in literacy, numeracy and for giving an excellent start to pupils' education. Secondary schools have been judged on inspection reports plus GCSE results.

Mr Chris Pickering, head-

Mr Pickering said no school could stay the same and that raising achievement was an on-going process.

That desire to continue moving forward was echoed by headteacher at Flintham Mrs Sheila Butler as well as Mr John Noden, headteacher at Chuter Ede.

emerged from that to lead his companions in a race from one vantage point to another above a picturesque valley. Below are some of the key events in his time as head:

2001 - County council submits a bid for PFI funding to rebuild Tuxford School

2002 - Successful application for Technology College status. New school uniform adopted: navy blue blazer, blue and gold tie. New diamond logo, new school motto and new aims introduced.

2005 - Construction of a new school began

2007 - The school moved into a new building and the group of old buildings were vacated then demolished. Training school status chosen by school in response to invitation to apply for a second technology specialism. History of Tuxford School published as part of the "*Landmark Year*" celebrations.

It soon became apparent that Chris Pickering's management style is to drive the school forward by identifying development targets before launching initiatives to meet the targets. Geoff Lloyd summarised the Pickering method: "Chris has employed 'scientific management' by setting agendas, establishing success criteria and collecting data. He has brought in effective monitoring and evaluation and the improvement plan is a vehicle to make sure certain things are moving forward.

"Chris sets a fast pace. Sometimes you feel overwhelmed and perhaps some of the early pace was too fast. Chris has done a good job of listening at meetings. He recognises the need to build slowly sometimes: that each step has to be really embedded. You don't want "new month, new initiative", we pick on one or two initiatives that need doing that are important and we push forward on those." (1)

Two early initiatives were the 'Whole Brain' Project (from 1997) and IQEA (from 1998). Geoff Lloyd and Tina Powell recruited enthusiastic teams of staff to introduce new teaching methods based on the two projects. The former encouraged students to improve thinking and note-taking skills whilst the latter, co-ordinated by Nottingham University, encouraged action research in schools to inform good practice: staff teams experimented with classroom seating arrangements, positive encouragement as a behaviour management strategy and so on. Testing of intake students to discover their natural ability was also introduced. Mr

Pickering informed governors in February: "Year 7 pupils have undertaken Cognitive Ability Tests (CATs) and this diagnostic assessment tool is allowing staff to identify areas of weakness and possible ways forward. The tests will also contribute to the school's monitoring and tracking system… The Whole Brain Project is making good progress and Year 7 pupils have now been involved in mind mapping exercises, brain fizzers and activities which raise self-esteem." (4)

Unfortunately the school budget was not as healthy as the curriculum. On 4 August 2000 the Newark Advertiser reported that the school had overspent by £52,386. The county council permitted some schools to overspend if there were good arguments for doing so, but overspending could not be sustained. A balanced budget was the aim. The report informed readers that sixteen county schools had overspent by more than £50,000 and that the Grove School in Balderton had overspent by £163,426: "Secondary schools with deficits over £20,000 and primary schools with deficits over £5,000 become licensed by the education authority with an agreed plan to bring the budget back in balance." Chairman of the education committee, Mr Mick Storey, was reported as saying that some redundancies would be unavoidable. (5)

Mr Pickering has been fortunate in being able to spend much more money on school development than his predecessor. Prime minister Tony Blair, when asked to identify his government's

Schools' staff cuts likely

TWO Advertiser area schools will be forced to review their staffing levels as a way of balancing their books. The Grove School, Balderton, overspent its budget by £163,426 in the last financial year, an annual report on school budget accounts to Nottinghamshire's education committee has revealed.

Tuxford School overspent by £52,386.

Sixteen county secondary schools have overspent by more than £50,000.

County education chiefs will start talks with head-teachers and school governors about how to reduce the deficits, but as staffing costs form the biggest part of school budgets teaching cuts look likely.

County education chairman Mr Mick Storey has conceded

some redundancies will be unavoidable. It is county policy to consider voluntary redundancies first.

Schools are finding it harder to balance their books, according to the report.

The number of primary schools overspending on budgets rose from 17 to 25 over the last financial year while the number of secondary schools overspending rose from 23 to 31.

Secondary schools with deficits over £20,000 and primary schools with deficits over £5,000 become licensed by the education authority with an agreed plan to bring the budget back in balance.

Reproduced courtesy of the *Newark Advertiser.* 4 Aug 2002.

priorities, famously declared them to be: "Education, education, education." Not only did the county put in a bid on the school's behalf for PFI funding to replace Tuxford's buildings (in December 2001) but also more money found its way into school – partially due to restraints being placed on the LEA's ability to withhold money from schools to cover county administration costs. A successful application for technology college status brought in an additional £500,000 over four years from April 2002. Bid co-ordinator Geoff Lloyd was pictured in a Retford Guardian report of the achievement: "To gain technology status the school had to raise £50,000 – a feat that took 18 months and involved several local companies, organisations, parents and friends. 'It was quite a formidable task, but as the target got closer we had a more concerted effort,' said Mr Lloyd." (6)

The additional resources were used for developments in information technology, design technology, maths and science. Additional staff were employed and additional equipment was purchased. The funding had been partly dependent upon making a commitment to assist other schools, mainly feeder primary schools. Tuxford computer technicians helped primary colleagues to set up systems and to master basic computing skills.

Mr Pickering next turned his attention to a review of how staff were deployed and managed at a time when there was a national debate about how teachers could become more effective. First the pastoral system at Tuxford (form tutors and year groups) was scrutinised and then

14 to 19 phase reception at the old school.

subject departments. From this investigation – and much discussion – emerged innovative solutions. In place of heads of year who were supposed to manage every aspect of a year group's behaviour, welfare and progress there would be teams of specialist welfare and progress managers who could focus on a specific area of responsibility. In each of the two phases - for students aged 11 to 14 and for those aged 14 to 19 - a specialist reception area was established from September 2002 and the phase managers were given administrative support from newly appointed phase secretaries.

A similar process for subject teachers led to the proposal that a single head of each department responsible for all curriculum decisions, exams, staff team building, etc would be replaced by a faculty team in which colleagues could specialise in student progress or development of teaching and learning. The mistakes of 1976 were avoided as large subject departments were simply renamed faculties. Historians and geographers joined together as Humanities and art, drama and music teachers were grouped in the Expressive and Creative Arts faculty. Individual staff within the faculties took on more responsibility, but it was targeted towards teaching and learning rather than buying stock, etc.

Geoff Lloyd recalled the process of change: "The current model of faculty took 18 months to debate and it came about because of workforce remodelling. We knew that teaching and learning responsibilities were coming in place of management responsibilities. What we weren't getting with the old pastoral and faculty systems was enough emphasis on progress and intervention. We needed to track progress across the faculty but it needed to go beyond just tracking to what we were going to do about the issues identified. We wanted to empower faculties with leadership to build up self-contained and supportive units. By putting people together they support each

148

other. The changes addressed a national issue but they were Tuxford's solution to the national agenda. It took a long time to put into place and there are still debates going on around that.

"The origin of change is often the national agenda, but it's a balance because in listening to staff we identify other issues. We come up with a Tuxford response and it's the Tuxford response that people under-estimate." (1)

In January 2003 a national agreement was signed by school workforce unions, local government employers and the government which would usher in a series of important changes to teachers' conditions of service and open the way for enhanced roles for school support staff. Teachers were to have time set aside for marking, they were to hand over administration to the experts and concentrate on teaching; in future they would be paid to teach, not to manage.

Planning for a replacement school building took Mr Pickering to many visits and meetings after the PFI funding was in place (from May 2002).

Mr Lloyd was asked to summarise some of the strengths of the school in 2007: "Compared to some schools, we still operate a high trust, low control model. If it's not going all right nobody goes down and 'has a word'. Instead we ask what support we can provide: what courses do you want to go on? do you want to go and visit another school? In that sense we trust them to get on with the job and it's only if it doesn't work that the Leadership Team has to get involved and ask questions such as why isn't it working? what can we do in the short term? what can we do in the long term? That's the way this school has always worked...

"Behaviour management has changed as well as syllabuses and we now know how to deal with the students more effectively. I think behaviour in the school today is as good as it ever has been... I'm not saying that it's correct all the time, we have some

Liz Briggs and John Gibson with a group of children in 2002, front cover of the 2002 school brochure.

Sam Page teaching in class.
Reproduced courtesy of the *Retford Times*.

Reproduced courtesy of the *Retford Times*. 13 Dec 2002.

Tea with Cherie

THE embattled Prime Minister's wife, Mrs Cherie Blair, took time away from her personal problems to chat with Tuxford School pupils on Tuesday.

Mrs Blair met the teenagers at Downing Street hours before appearing on national television to answer allegations about her dealings with a convicted fraudster.

Along with her husband, Mr Tony Blair, she chatted with pupils Jihan Ahmed (14) from Carlton-on-Trent, Kirsty Archer (15) from Elkesley and William Black (11) from Tuxford about their school and lessons.

Teacher Miss Julie Hethershaw, who accompanied the pupils, said Mrs Blair showed no sign of the furore that had surrounded her for the past week.

Leo Blair

She said: "She was very pleasant and delightful. Because she has children of her own she was very interested in what we had to say."

Even the couple's youngest son, Leo Blair, made an appearance at the event.

Mrs Blair had asked eight MPs, including the MP for Newark, Mr Patrick Mercer, to invite six constituents for tea at Downing Street.

Jihan, Kirsty and William were chosen to represent the school by staff and were accompanied to London by Miss Hethershaw, the school's social inclusion co-ordinator, Mrs Cheryl Stollery, and lunchtime supervisor Mrs Sally Black.

They arrived at Downing Street at 4.30pm and met the Blairs before having tea, biscuits and cakes.

The visit ended with a tour of the house.

● MR MERCER is pictured above outside Number 10 with the Tuxford party.

in Year 11 who wouldn't have been out of place 15 years ago - but then there is always that core. Results are an indicator, I suppose: we were getting mid 50 percentages achieving 5 or more A to C grade GCSEs, then we talked of 60 per cent and got 70 per cent last year. That must say something about the way we are going." (1)

Sources

1   *The Best Career Move I've Ever Made*, Geoff Lloyd, Tuxford School Archive Papers, unpublished, 2007

2   Photo and caption, Retford Times, 23 January 1997

3   *School among best in country*, Retford Times, 6 February 1997

4   *Headteacher's Report to Governing Body February 1998*, Chris Pickering, Tuxford School Archive Papers, unpublished

5   *School's staff cuts likely*, Newark Advertiser, 4 August 2000

6   *Tuxford School takes massive step forward*, Retford Guardian, 8 February 2002

2007 Staff Photograph – Surnames only.

Row 7 (Back) Baker, Williams, Kellington, Coalwood, Stockdale, Keeling, Tscherwatyi, Peacock, Griffiths, Evason, Reid, Bingham, Sloss, Mitchell, Coulson, Hardy, Curry, Cook.

Row 6 Lynch, Tsimbiridis, Peake, Taylor, Hannah, Stephen, Jones, Brightwell, Barr, Simpson, Thorpe, Vernon, Buck, Hardy.

Row 5 Lee, Creighton, Tivey, Jones, Hutchinson, Bland, Leathem-Pugh, Heathcote, Cook, Marsh, Jones, Stedham, Leachman, Burrell, Boneham, Garrett, Jones.

Row 4 Black, Peck, Rowland, Pashley, Roe, Mosley, Ward, Hallam, Ginever, Burton, Pearson.

Row 3 Chilvers, White, Walker, Dodd, Lee, Foster, Beresford, Footitt, Watson, Britton, Saxelby, Towle, Wilson, Merrills, Hirst, Higgins, Morfett, Machin.

Row 2 Gauntley, Evans, Fretwell, Hall, Jarman, Evans, Wright, Grant, Allport, Addison, Whitehead, Brumpton, Dickinson, Nichol, Maunder, Slack, Town.

Row 1 (Front) Lilley, Rew, Brammer, Hough, Wall, Crew, Powell, Lloyd, Pickering, Cotton, Madden, Hollingworth, Newstead, Hogan, Hethershaw.

On Task, On Target *The story of the first fifty years of Tuxford School*

Tuxford's Logos and School Mottos

1. Festina Lente (Success via Alternative Routes?)

The choice of Festina Lente as Tuxford School's motto for its first thirty one years seems strange now. Why choose a Latin phrase when the language was not taught in the school? Viewed in the context of the school's early classification as a secondary modern, the motto reveals a remarkably frank assessment of the students: a little slow but will get there in the end. It was government policy in the late 1950s that 80 per cent of all young people should "make haste slowly" in their education by taking a less academic road – the scenic route? - whilst the other 20 per cent made rapid advances on the educational highway in grammar schools. The policy was guided by good intentions, but was later criticised for being socially divisive. The policy makers had merely intended to base education on economic reality. As the work force consisted of relatively few "white collar workers" - members of the professions, managers and civil servants - with the skills to lead and a much larger number of skilled craftsmen and manual workers, it was argued that the education system would serve the country best by identifying and preparing the two distinct groups, separately, from as early an age as possible..

First headteacher, Bernard Woodward, chose the motto and he would be upset that such a cynical view could be taken of his choice because he was focusing on the rural nature of the school rather than its students' academic progress. He shared his reasoning with an audience of parents: "I think life in the country is still lived at something approximating to the right speed, and with this thought in mind the symbolism of our School Motto and Badge were selected. Our badge (as some of you will know) depicts the steady forward movement of the Stage Coach and the slow turning of the windmill sails using the elements to grind the grain, these set in a rural landscape, together with the motto 'Festina Lente' (hasten slowly) are I feel symbolical of a philosophy of education for Tuxford Rural Secondary School." Green and gold were chosen by Mr Woodward as the school colours as he regarded them as colours of the countryside.

The landscape badge was worn on blazers by early students, but a simplified close-up of the stagecoach was used on reports to parents. The choice of an old-fashioned stagecoach as Tuxford's logo could be interpreted today as a reflection of politically incorrect assumptions. Not only does it suggest that secondary modern students were seen to be taking the slow route but also were portrayed as unambitious in choice of transport and lacking energy – if the oversized sleeping passenger in the coach is representative. Of course, this is not the image that the logo was intended to convey. The positive interpretation would be a school proud to be part of the local community: proud of Tuxford's role in earlier centuries as a mailcoach staging post. Together the logo and motto represent he school as a group of people on a journey, moving forward steadily.

The early motto had another positive interpretation that was probably unknown to Mr Woodcock. Festina Lente was a favourite saying of the first Roman Emperor, Augustus Caesar. Scholars have argued that he was not interested in going slowly and that the broader meaning of lente has been missed in the translation. Augustus applied the paradox mostly to warfare and he meant "Success through Suppleness and Determination".

2. On Task, On Target

This was Keith Atkinson's favourite exhortation. On his many tours of the school, often in the company of suitably impressed visitors, he expected to see every student focusing on the lesson and its learning targets. The motto never replaced Festina Lente on school notepaper, but it was used every day in meetings and classrooms.

The stagecoach logo was replaced briefly from February 1997 to September 1999 by an idealised line drawing of the view from the hill above Tuxford windmill. A competition was organised by art teacher Peter Searle to design a new logo. The winning design was a collaborative effort by Charlene White and Mariell Barden. Heritage and technology were represented by St Nicholas Church, the mill, Marnham power station and the A1. The picture continues to have an important role as the masthead image on the school's termly newsletter for parents, Tuxford Topics.

Charlene White and Mariell Barden.

On Task, On Target *The story of the first fifty years of Tuxford School*

3. Excellence through Teamwork

The current logo and motto of Tuxford School were introduced in 2002 after a successful re-application for Charter Mark status. The corporate image of the school became a topic of discussion during the vetting process. The old image had to go and something more appropriate was needed. "Continuing Excellence" had been used as a strapline on a series of discussion papers published by Chris Pickering soon after his appointment as headteacher, but the phrase didn't quite reflect the whole range of school aims. Several alternatives were considered before Excellence through Teamwork was adopted. It reflects both the school's high aspirations and its preferred method of working.

The blue diamond logo, bearing a cream coloured S entwined around a golden T, was chosen to convey high quality and high value. The colour was chosen to match the new school uniform. Blue was considered more practical and tasteful than the previous green. However gold was retained as the subsidiary colour.

New smart look for brighter pupils

TUXFORD School pupils will be arriving at school next term in a new uniform.

The new style clothes have dropped the old colours in favour of a completely new design.

The old grey, green and gold colours have been replaced with mainly blue and will be worn by pupils as of September.

Assistant headteacher at Tuxford School, Mr Baker, said the new design was part of a new way forward for the school.

The old uniform has been worn by pupils since the school became a comprehensive back in 1976.

But recently, after the school gained technical college status, changes to the uniform were also drawn up.

Mr Baker said: "In future blue will be our school colour and from September blazers will be phased in as part of our drive to smarten the appearance of pupils.

"We believe that when pupils take pride in their appearance and in the school they will be more determined to succeed in other ways too."

Also to go is the schools old logo which has been replaced with a diamond.

Mr Baker said: "The logo is in the form of a diamond to denote excellence, high value and high quality because these are the school's aspirations.

"The motto reflects the drive for excellence but also stresses teamwork."

He added: "Anyone who has visited the school will know how happy and purposeful the atmosphere is as we work together to get better and better."

Reproduced courtesy of the *Retford Times*. 8 Aug 2002.

The School Leaving Age
from 1880 to the Present

1880   Education Act Tightened the provisions of the 1876 Education Act. Insisted on compulsory attendance from 5-10 years. Penalised employers of children under 13 years who did not have a certificate that they had reached the educational standard required by the local bye-laws.

1893   Education Act Minimum leaving age raised to 11.

1899   Education Act Minimum leaving age raised to 12.

1900   Education Act No employment under fourteen without a certificate.

1918   Education Act Full-time education compulsory from 5 – 14 years. Abolished half-time schooling and exemptions such as early leaving in agricultural districts which the earlier system allowed.

1926   The Hadlow Report recommended raising the minimum leaving age to 15. The establishment of Secondary Modern Schools as alternatives to Grammar Schools was also recommended.

1936   Education Act The school leaving age to be raised to 15 as from September 1939. Not implemented because of Second World War.

1944   Education Act The leaving age was raised to 15, with special power given to the Minister to delay this for two years. Clause 35 also provided for it be raised to 16 by Order in Council 'as soon as it was practicable'.

1947   School leaving age raised to 15.

1964   The decision to raise the age to 16 was announced and preparations began.

1968   Raising of the school leaving age postponed until 1972-73.

1972   The leaving age was raised to 16.

Numbers on roll

Some records may give different figures for the student population. Both sets of figures will probably be accurate as it is normal for some students to leave or join throughout an academic year. Reasons for this fluctuation are varied: some students may simply wish to change schools for personal reasons. Families move house all the time or split up due to divorce or bereavement.

Date (Sept)	Main School	Sixth Form	Total	Date (Sept)	Main School	Sixth Form	Total
Mr Woodward's first year as head				Mr Atkinson's first year as head			
1958/59	314	--	314	1978/79	764	--	764
1960/61	360	--	360				
1961/62	421	--	421	First sixth form			
1962/63	402	--	402	1980/81	772	11	783
1963/64	389	--	389	1981/82	?	42	?
1964/65	385	--	385	1982/83	779	67	846
1966/67	379	--	379	1985/86	791	78	869
1967/68	370	--	370	1986/87	783	73	856
1968/69	401	--	401	1987/88	750	72	822
1969/70	395	--	395	1988/89	710	71	781
1971/72	393	--	393	1989/90	668	94	762
1972/73	397	--	397	1990/91	689	110	799
				1991/92	708	111	819
First full fifth year (Y11)				1992/93	743	126	869
1973/74	498	--	498	1993/94	792	116	908
1974/75	528	--	528	1994/95	836	114	950
1975/76	585	--	585	1995/96	833	148	981
First comprehensive intake				Mr Pickering's first year as head			
1976/77	685	--	685	1996/97	848	166	1014
1977/78	740	--	740	1997/98	857	160	1017
				1998/99	857	160	1017
				1999/00	901	151	1052
				2000/01	909	159	1068
				2001/02	916	178	1094
				2004/05	973	233	1206
				2005/06	1028	228	1256
				Year of move from old school to new.			
				2006/07	1017	243	1260

Index

157

On Task, On Target *The story of the first fifty years of Tuxford School*